5-ingredient
COOKING
FOR TWO

5-ingredient
COOKING
FOR TWO

100+ RECIPES PORTIONED FOR PAIRS

BY ROBIN DONOVAN

CALLISTO PUBLISHING

Copyright © 2020 by Callisto Publishing LLC
Cover and internal design © 2020 by Callisto Publishing LLC
Interior photography © 2020 Evi Abeler.
Food styling by Albane Sharrard.
Cover photo by Nadine Greeff/Stocksy United.
Art Director: Jennifer Hsu
Art Producer: Megan Baggott
Editor: Anne Lowrey
Production Manager: Riley Hoffman
Production Editor: Melissa Edeburn

Published by Callisto Publishing LLC C/O Sourcebooks LLC
P.O. Box 4410, Naperville, Illinois 60567-4410
(630) 961-3900
callistopublishing.com

Printed and bound in China.
OGP 19

For Doug, my favorite plus-one

CONTENTS

INTRODUCTION

Like many people, I wear a lot of hats. In my professional life, I'm a small-business owner, a writer, an editor, a recipe developer, a blogger, and more. At home, I'm a wife, mother, grocery shopper, cook, driver, laundry-doer, cleaner-upper, and a million other things. No matter the number of roles we take on, it seems we're all busy. And even those of us who love to cook (raised hand!) need to keep meals simple if we're going to get them on the table. That's why I love five-ingredient cooking for two.

My family is small. There are just three of us—me, my husband, and my 11-year-old son—and my husband eats a pretty strict gluten-free, dairy-free diet, which my son and I do not follow. So when I cook for us as a family, I'm usually cooking one meal for myself and my son and a variation of it for my husband. (Yes, it's complicated!) As a result, I prefer to cook in small batches, and if I can simplify recipes to use only a handful of ingredients, all the better.

This book provides simple yet delicious recipes that make *just* enough for two. With small-batch cooking, you don't have to eat the same thing day after day or feel guilty about leftovers going to waste. Small-batch cooking saves money and helps you eat healthy-size portions.

Every recipe in this book, whether a breakfast option, a dinner entrée, a dessert, or a snack, uses just five ingredients. (Note: Cooking oil, salt, pepper, and water are not considered ingredients because they're often on hand and almost always needed.)

In addition to recipes, this book offers cooking tips and ideas for ingredient substitutions, equipment and cooking hacks, advice for shopping for ingredients in small quantities, and ways to use any leftovers.

Let's get cooking!

Chapter One

COOKING FOR TWO MADE SIMPLE

Scaling down recipes isn't always as easy as cutting the ingredients by half or three-quarters, but it is possible to make most of the dishes you love with fewer servings. A bit of know-how for shopping for ingredients in small quantities and some tips and tricks for small-batch cooking are all you need to get started.

GROCERY SHOPPING FOR TWO

Grocery shopping for two can pose nearly as many challenges as cooking for two. Supermarkets tend to sell food in quantities designed for families of four or more. Even when small packages are available, they're not always cost-effective. You either spend more money than you'd like or deal with leftover ingredients.

Here are a few ways you can minimize cost and waste:

1. Pantry staples like all-purpose flour, sugar (including granulated, powdered, and brown), dried beans, rice, and pasta are more economical when purchased in large quantities. These ingredients will last a long time in your cupboards, so you might as well cash in on the cost-effectiveness of large packages.

2. Buy produce loose whenever possible so that you can get just what you need. Some stores sell fruits and vegetables in bags or other packages so that you're forced to buy six apples when you only need two. For fruits and vegetables that you'll likely *not* snack on or use in multiple recipes, find a store that allows you to buy just what you need. Alternatively, if you end up with more fresh produce than you can use, you can freeze it instead of letting it go to waste.

3. Buy some fruits and vegetables frozen. A large package of frozen berries, peaches, peas, green beans, or corn can be kept in the freezer for months.

4. Meats are often cheaper when purchased in bulk, and most meats freeze well. Try buying a giant pack of chicken thighs, splitting them into single-recipe portions, and popping them in the freezer in freezer-safe containers.

5. When buying perishable ingredients—like eggs, sour cream, and cream cheese—don't make the mistake of trying to save money by buying them in large packages at a low cost per unit. For instance, if you need ¼ cup sour cream, buy the smallest possible container, unless sour cream is an ingredient you use often.

6. Look for ingredients in single-serving containers. Some ingredients, like yogurt, applesauce, juices, and milk, are commonly sold this way. By buying only what you need, you reduce food waste (and your grocery bill).

WHEN TO BUY IN BULK

As mentioned on the opposite page, some foods store well, either in the freezer or in the pantry, so it makes sense to cash in on savings by buying in bulk. Other foods, though, don't keep well, so in the long run, buying in bulk will end up costing you more rather than less when you're only shopping and storing for two.

DO BUY IN BULK

All-purpose flour

Dried beans

Dried pasta

Frozen fruits and vegetables

Granulated sugar

Meat

Unsalted butter

DON'T BUY IN BULK

Baked goods

Dairy products

Eggs

Fresh fruits and vegetables

Nuts

WHEN TO INVEST IN THE BEST

The challenge of cooking meals with just five ingredients is to make each ingredient count in terms of both flavor and satisfying your appetite. One of the best ways to ensure that each of your ingredients really shines is to find and invest in the highest-quality ingredients.

Pay attention to what is in season. Buying in-season produce is economical, and you'll get those fruits and vegetables at their peak. Opting for locally made or produced products is often another way to ensure that you are getting the best-quality ingredients.

The following items are particularly worthwhile investments:

- Butter
- Canned or smoked fish
- Cheese
- Chocolate
- Olive oil
- Vinegar

STORE SMARTER

When you're cooking—and shopping—for two, you're bound to end up with an excess of certain ingredients, leftovers, or both. Here are some tips for optimal food storage:

1. Grains, such as flour, rice, and oats, are best stored in airtight containers in a cool, dry place. Most grains will last at least six months if stored properly.

2. Leftovers can be stored in the refrigerator or freezer. Refrigerate them if you're going to eat them in the next few days; otherwise, freeze them. Either way, divide them first into serving-size portions, then wrap them well in plastic wrap or put them in airtight storage containers. Most leftovers will keep in the refrigerator for up to three days or in the freezer for three months.

3. Spices will best maintain their freshness and flavor when stored in airtight containers in a cool, dark place. The shelf life of spices varies, but spices can typically be stored from one to four years (whole spices last the longest).

4. Oils, such as olive, canola, or sesame, should also be stored in a cool, dark place and in airtight containers to prevent oxidation.

5. Fresh herbs, like basil, mint, and cilantro, are best stored in the refrigerator with their stems in a glass of water and their tops loosely covered by a plastic bag. If space is an issue, wrap fresh herbs in damp paper towels, tuck them into plastic bags, and store them in your refrigerator's vegetable drawer.

6. Store cut fruit and fresh berries covered in the refrigerator.

7. Whole fruit, such as oranges and apples, will best maintain their flavor if stored on the countertop and eaten within a few days of purchase.

8. If you have more fruit than you can eat in a few days, store it in the refrigerator. You may lose some of the flavor, but the fruit won't turn bad before you can eat it.

WHAT TO KEEP IN THE FREEZER

When freezing foods, be sure to use storage containers that are designated as freezer safe. Always mark the containers with the date and contents before you put them in the freezer. Here are my top tips for freezing various foods:

1. Meat, chicken, fish, and seafood freeze extremely well. Divide uncooked meat into recipe-size portions. Wrap each portion tightly in plastic wrap before placing it in a freezer-safe resealable plastic bag. Meat will keep in the freezer for at least three months. Thaw frozen meat in the refrigerator overnight before using.

2. Berries, peaches, nectarines, apricots, pineapples, mangos, and other similar fruits freeze especially well. To freeze, wash the fruit well and let it air-dry. Berries are best frozen whole. Peaches, nectarines, and apricots can be cut into wedges before freezing. Peel pineapples and mangos, discard the cores/pits, and cut the fruit into chunks to store. Freeze fruit in freezer-safe resealable plastic bags for three to six months.

3. Butter can be frozen right in the box, or you can freeze individual sticks in their original wrappers. Butter will keep in the freezer indefinitely.

4. Nuts are high in fat, which can go rancid if stored at room temperature for long periods. Store them in resealable plastic bags in the freezer indefinitely.

5. Eggs can be frozen for up to three months, though not in their shells. To freeze whole eggs, crack them, whisk the whites and yolks together, and pour the mixture into a freezer-safe storage container. You can also freeze egg whites and yolks separately. Multiple egg whites can be frozen in a freezer-safe container; individual egg whites can be frozen in the wells of an ice cube tray and transferred to a resealable plastic bag. Egg yolks need to have either salt or sugar added to them before freezing—for every four yolks, whisk in ⅛ teaspoon salt or 1½ teaspoons sugar. Like egg whites, egg yolks can be stored individually or in multiples and kept in the freezer for up to six months.

6. Dairy products—including milk, cream, half-and-half, and buttermilk—will expand as they freeze, so leave extra room in the container. I like to put these ingredients into freezer-safe resealable plastic bags and freeze them flat on a baking sheet. They are easy to store this way, and you can pre-measure the ingredients and mark the quantity on the bag before freezing. Dairy products will keep in the freezer for up to six months.

7. Cheese can be frozen, although it may be crumblier after thawing. I prefer to freeze shredded cheese and use it for cooking after thawing, in which case I don't notice the texture difference. Cheese can be kept frozen for up to six months.

Minimizing Food Waste

Even when employing your savviest shopping-for-two and food-storage strategies, you're bound to end up with some extra ingredients. Although I've designed these recipes with portion size and ingredient use in mind, you can find ideas for using leftover ingredients by looking through the index for other dishes that also use those foods (see page 168).

Here are my best general tips for repurposing leftovers:

- Extra bread can be turned into bread crumbs (either in a food processor or using a knife the old-fashioned way). You can toast them or not. Either way, store them in a resealable plastic bag in the freezer indefinitely, and use them as you would any bread crumbs when they are called for in a recipe.

- If you only need, say, half an onion for your recipe, go ahead and chop the whole thing. Store half of it in a resealable plastic bag in the refrigerator and use it for another recipe in the next few days. Or pop it in the freezer, where it will keep for up to 6 months.

- If you have more fresh herbs than you can use, chop them in a food processor with a bit of olive oil, then freeze the mixture in small portions in an ice cube tray. Use the cubes to add flavor to sauces and other dishes. (By the way, this method works for many sauces, especially pesto.)

- Store extra broth by freezing it flat in freezer-safe resealable plastic bags. This saves you freezer space, too.

- Store extra milk, cream, or buttermilk the same way—frozen flat in freezer-safe resealable plastic bags.

ESSENTIAL KITCHEN TOOLS FOR TWO

When you're cooking for two, you don't need bulky equipment, a large oven, or even a large kitchen. You can choose small equipment designed for small-batch cooking. For the recipes in this book, the equipment needs are minimal. Essential cooking tools include a sharp knife, a cutting board, an 8- or 10-inch nonstick skillet, a medium saucepan, a baking sheet, a loaf pan, and utensils, such as a wooden spoon, slotted spoon, and spatula. A microwave is handy for melting butter and chocolate and for reheating leftovers, but it is not essential.

You can use your regular-size equipment for most dishes, but if you are stocking a new kitchen and want to start out with small tools, here is a list of items you might like to have:

A 5-by-3-inch loaf pan is useful for making small cakes and quick breads, meatloaf, or casserole-type dishes like lasagna or enchiladas.

A countertop convection oven can stand in for a full-size electric or gas oven and can even be used as a toaster.

A mini food processor, like the Cuisinart Mini-Prep or a bullet-style blender, is great for chopping garlic and herbs or pureeing ingredients for sauces.

A rimmed 9-by-13-inch baking sheet is perfect for making one-pan meals.

THE 5-INGREDIENT PANTRY

In creating the recipes for this book, I've attempted to minimize the number of ingredients you'll need to purchase. To that end, many ingredients—especially those you may not already have in your pantry—appear in multiple recipes. In the lists that follow, I've shared some of the staples you'll find most frequently used in the recipes in this book.

OILS AND FATS

Butter (unsalted is my preference—that way, you can have more control over how salty your dish is)

Cooking oil (any neutral-flavored, high-smoke-point oil like canola, sunflower seed, or safflower)

Olive oil (extra-virgin is the best for cooking and also has great flavor for use in salad dressings and as a finishing oil)

Sesame oil

DRY GOODS

All-purpose flour (the recipes in this book use only all-purpose flour)

Baking powder

Baking soda

Oats (old-fashioned rolled)

Sugar (granulated, brown, and powdered, also called confectioners')

SEASONINGS

Black pepper

Cayenne pepper

Chili powder

Cumin (ground)

Italian seasoning

Kosher salt

Oregano (dried)

Red pepper flakes

Soy sauce

FRESH HERBS

Basil

Chives

Cilantro

Parsley (flat-leaf)

Thyme

DAIRY AND EGGS

Cream cheese

Heavy (whipping) cream

Large eggs

Milk

Meal Planning

Planning meals for a week or even a month can help you save a ton of time and effort and will help you use leftover ingredients before they go bad. Here is my basic process:

1. **Write a schedule** for every meal you plan to prepare over the period for which you wish to plan. Include meals out and snacks if you like.

2. **Decide on a couple of recipes** you'd like to make. You can fill in your schedule with other recipes that use some of the same ingredients.

3. **Put each recipe into your schedule.** If you are planning to make one or more of the recipes in advance, mark down both when you plan to cook it and when you plan to serve it. If you plan to make large portions, schedule meals for the leftovers that you don't plan to freeze.

4. **Make shopping lists.** Go through each recipe and write down all the ingredients you need to purchase. While you are doing this, check the quantities of pantry items you already have to ensure that you have enough for every recipe you plan to cook.

5. **Do your shopping** and any food preparation.

SIMPLE COOKING HACKS

Five-ingredient recipes are great for simplifying both cooking and shopping. Here are some of my favorite cooking hacks to guarantee these recipes are extra flavorful and satisfying.

SPICE BLENDS

One of the biggest complaints I hear is that a recipe requires cooks to purchase many spices, some of which they never use again. Spice mixtures like chili powder, typically a mixture of ground chiles, paprika, cumin, coriander, and oregano, eliminate this frustration. You can buy these spice blends premade from your super-market or make them yourself.

These are a few of my favorite spice mixtures and the spices they typically include:

Chili powder: Cayenne pepper, cumin, dried chiles, garlic powder, oregano, paprika

Chinese 5-spice powder: Cinnamon, cloves, fennel, star anise, Szechuan peppercorns

Curry powder: Coriander, cumin, dried chiles, fenugreek, turmeric

Garam masala: Bay leaves, cardamom, cinnamon, cloves, coriander, cumin, dried chiles, fennel, nutmeg, peppercorns, mace

Italian seasoning: Basil, marjoram, oregano, rosemary, thyme

Pumpkin pie spice: Allspice, cinnamon, cloves, ginger, nutmeg

OPTIONAL FINISHING TOUCHES

Although the recipes in this book adhere strictly to the five-ingredient limit, I have included some optional finishing touches throughout to allow for greater versatility when and if you want it. These touches are easy to implement and add flavor or visual flair. Some of my favorites are simple garnishes—a sprinkling of a chopped fresh herb like parsley or thyme, a drizzle of a flavored oil like chili oil or toasted sesame oil, a dollop of something like whipped cream, sour cream, or applesauce, or a sprinkling of chopped nuts or grated cheese.

KITCHEN SHORTCUTS

Let's face it, none of us has hours to spend in the kitchen. And if you've gotten your-self a copy of a book called *5-Ingredient Cooking for Two*, I'm willing to bet that you are especially interested in getting in and out of the kitchen quickly.

Here are a few of my favorite kitchen shortcuts:

Combine cooking processes. Instead of roasting a chicken in the oven and sau-téing vegetables on the stovetop, choose dishes that can be cooked together. For instance, roast vegetables right alongside the chicken.

Clean as you go. Yes, your mother was right about this one. Clutter and mess in your workspace will only slow you down. Keep your workspace as tidy as possible, and your cooking process will be so much smoother.

Prepare for the day and week ahead. If you need half an onion diced for tonight's dinner, look at your meal schedule to determine whether you'll need another half an onion diced for another recipe (hint: you will). Dice the whole onion and store the extra in a resealable plastic bag in the refrigerator. Same goes for garlic, fresh ginger, and any other ingredients you use frequently.

Buy some ingredients in prepped form. For instance, if you tend to use a lot of shredded Cheddar cheese, purchase a bag of the preshredded stuff. Some vegeta-bles, like butternut squash, sweet potatoes, green beans, and Brussels sprouts, can be found in supermarket produce sections already trimmed and cut. Mixed salad greens come prewashed and ready to toss in a bowl with your dressing.

Three words: *mise en place* ("put in place"). Having your ingredients ready to go before you begin cooking allows you to easily throw them into the pan when needed. This preparation will be your number one time and sanity saver in the kitchen.

Simple Ways to Add Flavor

Some recipes rely on long cooking times, complicated steps, and numerous ingredients to add flavor. But there are lots of ways you can elevate the flavor of a dish that don't take a lot of extra time or effort. Here are my top kitchen tips and tricks:

1. **Roast.** High, dry heat develops intense flavor and caramelizes sugars in meat and vegetables.

2. **Sear.** Even when you are cooking meat by a moist method like braising, you can develop intense layers of flavor by first seasoning then searing it in a hot pan. This method both caramelizes the outside of the meat and seals in the meat's juices and natural flavor.

3. **Caramelize.** Similar to roasting, caramelizing is a technique for drawing out the natural sugars in foods (vegetables and fruits all have natural sugars) and browning them. This technique concentrates sweetness and gives food a rich, nutty, toasty flavor.

4. **Add salt.** Salt isn't just meant to make food *salty*. It actually draws out and balances a food's natural flavors. The maxim "salt early and often" is a good one to remember. Add salt to your dishes at the beginning of cooking, the end of cooking, and at several points in between. You don't need to go crazy by dumping in a whole lot. Add a little, taste, and add a little more. For best results, use a good quality salt without additives like anti-caking compounds. Pure sea salt and kosher salt are the best options because they are unadulterated and provide clean salt flavor.

→

5. **Use fresh spices.** For the best flavor, keep your spices whole and grind them yourself just before using them. If doing so is too much trouble—believe me, I get it—buy spices in quantities that you'll use within a few months. And get a good peppermill because freshly ground pepper is the best!

6. **Consider adding citrus before serving.** Squeeze a bit of lemon or lime juice into a soup or sauce just before serving to brighten a dish and add balance when the dish is sweet or salty.

7. **Don't avoid fat.** Fat infuses your dish with flavor, so whether you are using butter, olive oil, coconut oil, or bacon fat, don't skimp on it. Drizzle additional olive oil or seasoned butter over your dishes for a flavorful final touch.

8. **Use a mix of cheeses rather than one cheese.** When a dish calls for shredded cheese, use a mix. An Italian cheese mix, which might include mozzarella, fontina, Asiago, and Parmesan, makes a super-flavorful pizza topping.

9. **Try all-in-one seasoning ingredients.** Use seasoning mixes or ready-made sauces, such as salsas, hot sauces, Worcestershire sauce, or barbecue sauce, to add multiple flavors with one ingredient.

ABOUT THE RECIPES

I have designed the recipes in this book to deliver flavor and satisfaction with only five or fewer ingredients. I haven't resorted to condensed soups or jarred Alfredo sauce. In general, the recipes call for whole foods, using mostly fresh ingredients (with exceptions like canned diced tomatoes and frozen peas and corn, which are greatly convenient and don't compromise taste). If these recipes have a "trick," it's using flavorful ingredients and simple but effective cooking techniques for enhancing flavor.

The recipes use many of the same ingredients to simplify shopping and minimize waste, but, collectively, they also provide variety so that you don't get bored in the kitchen.

Recipe labels will help you find dishes that you can make quickly and those that are easiest to prep for the week ahead:

30 MINUTES OR LESS   **30 Minutes or Less** recipes can be made in no more than half an hour.

FEELING FANCY   **Feeling Fancy** recipes are perfect for a romantic meal or cooking for company.

FREEZER-FRIENDLY   **Freezer-Friendly** recipes can be made in advance and saved for those times when you just aren't able to cook.

ONE PAN / ONE POT   **One Pan/One Pot** recipes use just one cooking vessel, which means fewer dishes to wash.

I've also included six types of tips to help you get the most out of the recipes and also to customize them:

Cooking Tips streamline prep and cooking or developing flavors.

Optional Finishing Touches are tips for simple toppings or garnishes added at the end of the cooking process.

Storage Tips minimize waste and make prepping and saving food a breeze.

Variations offer ingredient substitutions or other modifications to a dish.

Flavor Tips are my suggestions for intensifying flavor.

Pairing Tips identify foods and drink that work well with a given dish.

Baked Eggs with Spinach and Goat Cheese, page 24

Chapter Two

BREAKFAST

PBJ SMOOTHIE

30 MINUTES OR LESS

SERVES 2 / PREP TIME: 5 MINUTES

Frozen berries and peanut butter flavor this smoothie that's perfect for those days when you don't have time to sit down and eat. Pack these to go before the two of you head out of the house for the day.

1½ CUPS REDUCED-FAT MILK

1½ CUPS FROZEN
   BERRIES (RASPBERRIES,
   STRAWBERRIES,
   BLUEBERRIES,
   BLACKBERRIES, OR A MIX)

1 BANANA

2 TABLESPOONS
   PEANUT BUTTER

2 TABLESPOONS HONEY

In a blender, combine the milk, berries, banana, peanut butter, and honey, and blend until smooth. Serve immediately.

Variation: Peaches or mango would be delicious substitutes for berries.

Per serving: Calories: 347; Total Fat: 10g; Saturated Fat: 3g; Cholesterol: 9mg; Sodium: 155mg; Total Carbohydrates: 56g; Sugars: 43g; Protein: 12g

RASPBERRY OVERNIGHT OATS WITH TOASTED COCONUT AND ALMONDS

SERVES 2 / PREP TIME: 5 MINUTES, PLUS OVERNIGHT TO CHILL

Overnight oats make for a healthy breakfast and are really convenient and easy to prepare. Before bed, mix the oats and milk; the next morning, stir in some jam and sprinkle with nuts and coconut. You can even make a big batch, so you'll have enough for several days. Make individual portions in mason jars, which are great to take on the go.

1 CUP OLD-FASHIONED ROLLED OATS

1 CUP REDUCED-FAT MILK

4 TABLESPOONS RASPBERRY JAM

4 TABLESPOONS UNSWEETENED COCONUT FLAKES, TOASTED

2 TABLESPOONS CHOPPED TOASTED ALMONDS

1. In a medium bowl, stir together the oats and milk. Cover the bowl and refrigerate overnight.

2. To serve, divide the oat mixture into two individual serving bowls. Swirl 2 tablespoons of the jam into each bowl, then sprinkle the coconut and almonds over the top, dividing the ingredients equally between both servings.

Variation: Substitute any jam, preserves, fresh fruit, or nut butter you like for the raspberry jam.

Per serving: Calories: 419; Total Fat: 13g; Saturated Fat: 6g; Cholesterol: 6mg; Sodium: 85mg; Total Carbohydrates: 66g; Sugars: 27g; Protein: 11g

STRAWBERRY AND BRIE FRENCH TOAST SANDWICHES

30 MINUTES OR LESS **FEELING FANCY**

SERVES 2 / PREP TIME: 5 MINUTES / COOK TIME: 5 MINUTES

Because sometimes you're unsure if you want a savory breakfast or a sweet one, this recipe combines both. These breakfast sandwiches elevate French toast to a whole new level. If you like protein to start the day, put a slice of ham or a couple slices of cooked bacon in each sandwich before cooking.

2 OUNCES BRIE
  CHEESE, SLICED

4 SANDWICH BREAD SLICES

¼ CUP STRAWBERRY
  PRESERVES OR
  STRAWBERRY JAM

2 LARGE EGGS, BEATEN

2 TEASPOONS
  REDUCED-FAT MILK

NONSTICK COOKING SPRAY

1. Divide the Brie slices between two of the slices of bread. Top with the strawberry preserves, then place the remaining bread slices on top.

2. In a wide, shallow bowl, whisk together the eggs and milk.

3. Spray a large nonstick skillet with cooking spray and heat over medium heat.

4. Dunk the sandwiches into the egg mixture, coating both sides well.

5. Cook the sandwiches in the skillet for 2 to 3 minutes per side, until golden brown. Serve hot.

Optional Finishing Touch: Sprinkle powdered sugar over the sandwiches before serving.

Flavor Tip: Use an egg bread like challah or brioche instead of sandwich bread for extra richness.

Per serving: Calories: 420; Total Fat: 15g; Saturated Fat: 7g; Cholesterol: 215mg; Sodium: 528mg; Total Carbohydrates: 51g; Sugars: 23g; Protein: 20g

APPLE CINNAMON PANCAKES

30 MINUTES OR LESS

SERVES 2 / PREP TIME: 5 MINUTES / COOK TIME: 5 MINUTES

This recipe dresses up store-bought pancake mix with the flavors of cinnamon and apple. Try serving these pancakes with a dollop of vanilla yogurt instead of syrup.

⅔ CUP BUTTERMILK
   PANCAKE MIX
½ TEASPOON GROUND
   CINNAMON
⅔ CUP APPLESAUCE
1½ TABLESPOONS
   REDUCED-FAT MILK
NONSTICK COOKING SPRAY
MAPLE SYRUP, FOR SERVING

1. In a medium bowl, stir together the pancake mix and cinnamon. Stir in the applesauce and milk. Mix well.

2. Spray a large skillet with cooking spray and ladle the batter into the skillet, using about ¼ cup batter per pancake. When the pancakes begin to bubble on top and their edges start to firm, flip them and cook for 2 to 3 minutes more, until golden brown on the second side.

3. Serve hot, drizzled with maple syrup.

Pairing Tip: For even more concentrated apple flavor, sauté a diced apple with butter in a separate skillet until softened. Add 1 tablespoon brown sugar and cook, stirring, until the sugar is completely melted and the liquid thickens. Spoon over the pancakes.

Per serving: Calories: 221; Total Fat: 2g; Saturated Fat: 1g; Cholesterol: 6mg; Sodium: 219mg; Total Carbohydrates: 51g; Sugars: 36g; Protein: 3g

BREAKFAST QUESADILLAS

30 MINUTES OR LESS

SERVES 2 / PREP TIME: 5 MINUTES / COOK TIME: 15 MINUTES

Quesadillas are a tasty, fuss-free dinner option. Add scrambled eggs, and they make a protein-packed breakfast that will keep you satisfied until lunch.

4 LARGE EGGS

1 TABLESPOON
  REDUCED-FAT MILK

KOSHER SALT

FRESHLY GROUND
  BLACK PEPPER

1 TABLESPOON
  UNSALTED BUTTER

2 (10-INCH) FLOUR
  TORTILLAS

½ CUP SHREDDED
  MONTEREY JACK CHEESE

NONSTICK COOKING SPRAY

1. In a medium bowl, whisk together the eggs, milk, and salt and pepper to taste.

2. In a medium nonstick skillet, melt the butter over medium-high heat. Add the eggs and cook, stirring frequently, for 2 to 3 minutes, until set. Transfer the eggs to a plate or bowl.

3. Sprinkle half the cheese over one tortilla in an even layer. Top with the cooked eggs, then the remaining cheese. Place the second tortilla on top.

4. Wipe out the skillet you used to cook the eggs, then spray with cooking spray and heat over medium-high heat.

5. Cook the quesadilla in the skillet for 3 to 5 minutes, until golden brown on the bottom. Carefully flip it over and cook until the second side is golden brown and the cheese is melted, about 3 minutes more.

6. Remove the quesadilla from the pan and let it stand for a few minutes before slicing it into eight wedges.

7. Divide the quesadilla wedges between two plates and serve.

Optional Finishing Touch: Top with sour cream, salsa, sliced avocado, sliced scallions, or hot sauce, as preferred.

Flavor Tip: For a spicy kick, use pepper Jack instead of Monterey Jack cheese.

Per serving: Calories: 518; Total Fat: 30g; Saturated Fat: 13g; Cholesterol: 413mg; Sodium: 897mg; Total Carbohydrates: 38g; Sugars: 3g; Protein: 25g

BAKED EGGS WITH SPINACH AND GOAT CHEESE

30 MINUTES OR LESS　　**FEELING FANCY**

SERVES 2 / PREP TIME: 5 MINUTES / COOK TIME: 10 MINUTES

Baking eggs in individual ramekins, with just a drizzle of heavy cream, makes a simple breakfast seem special. Adding spinach, goat cheese, and fresh herbs further elevates this dish. Feel free to use different vegetables, cheeses, or herbs, but keep the order of ingredients intact: veggies and cheese on the bottom, eggs in the middle, and cream and seasonings on top.

NONSTICK COOKING
　SPRAY OR BUTTER, FOR
　PREPARING THE RAMEKINS

½ CUP CHOPPED
　BABY SPINACH

1½ OUNCES GOAT CHEESE

2 LARGE EGGS

2 TABLESPOONS HEAVY
　(WHIPPING) CREAM

1 TEASPOON CHOPPED
　FRESH HERBS (BASIL,
　THYME, OR OREGANO)

KOSHER SALT

FRESHLY GROUND
　BLACK PEPPER

TOASTED WHOLE-WHEAT
　OR SOURDOUGH BREAD,
　FOR SERVING (OPTIONAL)

1. Preheat the oven to 375°F and spray 2 (6-ounce) ramekins with cooking spray.

2. Add half the spinach to each ramekin, then crumble the cheese on top, dividing it equally.

3. Crack an egg into each ramekin. Pour 1 tablespoon of the cream over each egg. Sprinkle the herbs over the top of each ramekin, and season with salt and pepper.

4. Bake for 8 to 12 minutes, until the egg whites are set but the yolk is still runny, and the cream bubbles around the edges.

5. Remove from the oven and let cool for a couple of minutes before serving.

6. Serve immediately, with toasted whole-wheat or sourdough bread, if desired.

Variation: Add diced tomatoes or diced roasted red bell peppers along with the goat cheese.

Per serving: Calories: 185; Total Fat: 15g; Saturated Fat: 8g; Cholesterol: 216mg; Sodium: 237mg; Total Carbohydrates: 2g; Sugars: 1g; Protein: 11g

CHORIZO AND EGG BREAKFAST BURRITOS

30 MINUTES OR LESS

SERVES 2 / PREP TIME: 5 MINUTES / COOK TIME: 10 MINUTES

These warm flour tortillas rolled around an egg, cheese, and spicy sausage filling are perfect for breakfast on a rushed weekday morning.

4 OUNCES CHORIZO, LOOSE
   OR REMOVED FROM
   ITS CASING
2 LARGE EGGS
2 TEASPOONS
   REDUCED-FAT MILK
PINCH KOSHER SALT
PINCH FRESHLY GROUND
   BLACK PEPPER
2 (8-INCH) FLOUR
   TORTILLAS, WARMED
¼ CUP SHREDDED
   CHEDDAR CHEESE

1. Heat a medium skillet over medium-high heat. Add the chorizo and cook, stirring and breaking up the meat with a spatula, for about 5 minutes, until browned. Drain the excess fat from the skillet.

2. In a small bowl, whisk together the eggs, milk, salt, and pepper. Add the egg mixture to the skillet with the chorizo and cook, stirring, for about 3 minutes, until the eggs are fully set.

3. Lay the tortillas on a work surface, and spoon half the egg mixture into the center of each tortilla. Sprinkle the cheese over the filling.

4. Fold the sides of each tortilla over the egg filling, then roll up the burrito from the bottom to the top. Serve immediately.

Optional Finishing Touch: Before rolling up the burritos, add chopped fresh cilantro, thinly sliced scallions, or salsa.

Variation: For a vegetarian version, substitute soy chorizo (which is just as delicious) for the chorizo.

Per serving: Calories: 532; Total Fat: 35g; Saturated Fat: 14g; Cholesterol: 251mg; Sodium: 1,229mg; Total Carbohydrates: 26g; Sugars: 2g; Protein: 27g

GREEK SCRAMBLE
BREAKFAST WRAPS

30 MINUTES OR LESS **FREEZER-FRIENDLY**

SERVES 2 / PREP TIME: 5 MINUTES / COOK TIME: 5 MINUTES

This simple egg, cheese, and veggie wrap has everything you want in a breakfast: plenty of protein and healthy carbs and tons of flavor. To speed up the prep, cook the spinach ahead of time and keep it in the refrigerator. When you're ready, warm up the spinach in the microwave while you scramble the eggs.

4 LARGE EGGS

KOSHER SALT

FRESHLY GROUND
  BLACK PEPPER

2 TABLESPOONS OLIVE
  OIL, DIVIDED

2 CUPS BABY SPINACH

2 (10-INCH) WHOLE-WHEAT
  TORTILLAS OR WRAPS

8 CHERRY
  TOMATOES, HALVED

1 CUP CRUMBLED
  FETA CHEESE

1. In a medium bowl, whisk together the eggs, salt and pepper to taste, and 1 tablespoon water.

2. In a medium nonstick skillet, heat 1 tablespoon of the olive oil over medium-high heat. Add the eggs and cook, stirring frequently, for 2 to 3 minutes, until set. Transfer the eggs to a plate or bowl.

3. Wipe out the skillet, add the remaining 1 tablespoon olive oil, and heat over medium heat. Add the spinach and cook, stirring frequently, for about 2 minutes, just until the spinach wilts. Transfer the spinach to a plate or bowl.

4. Wipe out the skillet again. Over medium-high heat, briefly heat the tortillas, one at a time, for about 30 seconds per side.

5. Lay the warm tortillas flat on a work surface. Add half the eggs, spinach, tomatoes, and cheese down the center of each tortilla.

6. Fold the sides of each tortilla over the egg filling, then roll up the wrap from the bottom to the top. Serve immediately.

Storage Tip: You can make a bunch of these wraps ahead of time, covering each one tightly with plastic wrap. Refrigerate for up to 3 days or freeze for up to 3 months. Thaw frozen wraps in the refrigerator overnight, then remove the plastic wrap, roll each wrap in a damp paper towel, and reheat for about 2 minutes in the microwave.

Per serving: Calories: 650; Total Fat: 42g; Saturated Fat: 15g; Cholesterol: 422mg; Sodium: 1,321mg; Total Carbohydrates: 43g; Sugars: 6g; Protein: 28g

LOX AND EGGS SANDWICHES

30 MINUTES OR LESS

SERVES 2 / PREP TIME: 5 MINUTES / COOK TIME: 5 MINUTES

Breakfast sandwiches made with smoky, salty lox and rich, cream cheese–filled scrambled eggs are both decadent and relatively healthy.

2 ENGLISH MUFFINS, SPLIT

2 TABLESPOONS SALTED
   BUTTER, DIVIDED

4 LARGE EGGS

KOSHER SALT

FRESHLY GROUND
   BLACK PEPPER

2 TABLESPOONS
   CREAM CHEESE

2 SLICES NOVA LOX

1. Toast the English muffins, then spread the cut sides with 1 tablespoon of the butter.

2. In a medium bowl, whisk together the eggs and salt and pepper to taste.

3. In a medium nonstick skillet, melt the remaining 1 tablespoon butter over medium-high heat. Add the eggs and cook, stirring frequently, until almost set, about 2 minutes. Fold the cream cheese into the eggs and cook for another minute or so, until the cheese is melted and the eggs are fully cooked. Remove the pan from the heat.

4. Equally divide the egg mixture between two of the English muffin halves. Drape one slice of lox over each, then top with a second English muffin half. Serve immediately.

Optional Finishing Touch: Try topping this sandwich with sliced tomato, chopped fresh dill, or thinly sliced red onion, or all of them together.

Flavor Tip: Add 1 tablespoon capers to the eggs along with the cream cheese to bring out the flavor further.

Per serving: Calories: 538; Total Fat: 32g; Saturated Fat: 16g; Cholesterol: 439mg; Sodium: 983mg; Total Carbohydrates: 44g; Sugars: 6g; Protein: 26g

SWEET POTATO HASH WITH BACON, EGGS, AND CHEESE

30 MINUTES OR LESS

SERVES 2 / PREP TIME: 5 MINUTES / COOK TIME: 20 MINUTES

This sweet and savory combination of sweet potatoes, bacon, creamy goat cheese, and eggs packs a flavor punch.

4 BACON SLICES

1 JEWEL OR GARNET SWEET POTATO OR YAM, PEELED AND DICED

½ ONION, DICED

KOSHER SALT

FRESHLY GROUND BLACK PEPPER

2 LARGE EGGS

2 OUNCES GOAT CHEESE

1. Heat a medium oven-safe skillet over medium-high heat. Cook the bacon for 3 to 4 minutes per side, until crisp. Transfer to a paper towel–lined plate. Crumble the bacon after it has cooled.

2. Remove all but about 1 tablespoon of the bacon fat from the skillet. Cook the sweet potato and onion in the bacon fat, stirring frequently, for 8 to 10 minutes, until the vegetables are softened and beginning to brown.

3. While the vegetables are cooking, preheat the broiler on high.

4. Stir the bacon into the vegetable mixture, season with salt and pepper, then spread the mixture into an even layer in the skillet. Make four small indentations in the vegetable mixture. Crack an egg into each indentation, and season with salt and pepper. Place the pan under the broiler and cook for 3 to 4 minutes, until the egg whites are set but the yolks are still runny.

5. Remove the skillet from the broiler and immediately crumble the cheese over the top. Serve hot.

Optional Finishing Touch: Sprinkle sliced fresh chives or chopped fresh cilantro over the hash. Or consider stirring a dollop of sour cream into the dish for added creaminess.

Per serving: Calories: 472; Total Fat: 31g; Saturated Fat: 14g; Cholesterol: 258mg; Sodium: 1,160mg; Total Carbohydrates: 17g; Sugars: 5g; Protein: 30g

TOMATO, ZUCCHINI, AND CHEESE FRITTATA

30 MINUTES OR LESS

SERVES 2 / PREP TIME: 5 MINUTES / COOK TIME: 15 MINUTES

A frittata filled with vegetables and cheese has all the flavors of an omelet but is less fussy. It tastes great hot, at room temperature, or chilled. Dress up this frittata by adding fresh herbs like basil, cilantro, thyme, or sage.

NONSTICK COOKING SPRAY

4 LARGE EGGS

½ TEASPOON KOSHER SALT

1 ZUCCHINI, SHREDDED ON THE LARGE HOLES OF A BOX GRATER

1 MEDIUM TOMATO, DICED

1 TABLESPOON FINELY CHOPPED FRESH CHIVES

½ CUP SHREDDED CHEDDAR CHEESE, DIVIDED

1. Preheat the oven to 400°F.

2. Spray a large oven-safe skillet with cooking spray and heat over medium-high heat.

3. In a medium bowl, whisk together the eggs and salt. Stir in the zucchini, tomato, chives, and ¼ cup of the cheese. Pour the egg mixture into the skillet, and sprinkle the remaining ¼ cup cheese on top. Let the mixture cook for 2 to 3 minutes, until the bottom begins to set.

4. Transfer the skillet to the oven and bake for 12 to 14 minutes, until the eggs are set. Remove the skillet from the oven and let rest for 5 minutes before slicing the frittata into wedges to serve. Serve hot, at room temperature, or chilled.

Variation: You can substitute 2 thinly sliced scallions for the chives if preferred or if scallions are more easily available.

Per serving: Calories: 287; Total Fat: 20g; Saturated Fat: 9g; Cholesterol: 402mg; Sodium: 910mg; Total Carbohydrates: 7g; Sugars: 4g; Protein: 21g

EGGS BENEDICT

30 MINUTES OR LESS **FEELING FANCY**

SERVES 2 / PREP TIME: 15 MINUTES / COOK TIME: 15 MINUTES

Eggs Benedict is no chore to make. It uses only a handful of ingredients and is simple to put together. The hardest part may be poaching the eggs to perfection.

4 SLICES CANADIAN BACON

2 EGG YOLKS

1½ TEASPOONS FRESHLY
   SQUEEZED LEMON JUICE

¼ TEASPOON KOSHER SALT

5 TABLESPOONS UNSALTED
   BUTTER, MELTED

4 LARGE EGGS

2 ENGLISH MUFFINS, SPLIT
   AND TOASTED

FRESHLY GROUND
   BLACK PEPPER

1. Place a medium saucepan or deep skillet filled with about 3 inches of water over high heat. This will be your egg-poaching pan.

2. In a large skillet, cook the Canadian bacon over medium-high heat for about 2 minutes per side, until it is sizzling and lightly browned. Remove the skillet from the heat.

3. To make the sauce, in a blender, combine the egg yolks, lemon juice, and salt. Blend on high speed for about 30 seconds, until the mixture lightens to a pale yellow. With the blender running at low speed, drizzle the melted butter into the mixture. Continue blending until the mixture is thick and well combined. If it is too thick, add a small amount of warm water to thin it.

4. When the egg-poaching water is boiling, reduce the heat to low and crack in the eggs carefully. Raise the heat a bit if needed—you want the water to be gently simmering, with some small bubbles around the eggs. Set a timer for 4 minutes.

5. To assemble the eggs Benedict, place a slice of Canadian bacon on top of each toasted English muffin half. Using a slotted spoon, carefully lift the eggs out of the water one at a time, letting the excess water drain. Place an egg on top of each muffin half.

6. Drizzle the sauce over the tops of the eggs, dividing it equally. Garnish with freshly ground pepper, and serve immediately.

Optional Finishing Touch: Sprinkle minced fresh chives over the top as a garnish before serving.

Variation: Substitute sliced lox (you may have some left over from the Lox and Eggs Sandwiches, page 28) for the Canadian bacon for a decadent twist on this classic dish.

Per serving: Calories: 702; Total Fat: 49g; Saturated Fat: 25g; Cholesterol: 698mg; Sodium: 1,647mg; Total Carbohydrates: 31g; Sugars: 4g; Protein: 37g

*Grilled Prosciutto and
Fig Sandwiches, page 46*

Chapter Three

SOUPS AND SANDWICHES

SPICY, CHEESY POTATO SOUP

30 MINUTES OR LESS   **ONE POT**

SERVES 2 / PREP TIME: 10 MINUTES / COOK TIME: 15 MINUTES

This simple soup might be the quickest way to get a bowl of comfort food on the table. By using a seasoning mixture that contains black and red pepper, garlic powder, and other spices, you add a lot of flavor without a lot of ingredients. You can use that same seasoning to flavor boiled, poached, or roasted seafood, eggs, potatoes, and all sorts of other dishes as well.

1 TABLESPOON OLIVE OIL

1 (15-OUNCE) PACKAGE FROZEN DICED POTATOES AND ONIONS, THAWED

4 CUPS LOW-SODIUM VEGETABLE BROTH

2 TEASPOONS CAJUN SEASONING (I LIKE TONY CHACHERE'S), PLUS MORE IF NEEDED

1 CUP WHOLE MILK

KOSHER SALT (OPTIONAL)

1 CUP SHREDDED SHARP CHEDDAR CHEESE, PLUS ADDITIONAL FOR GARNISH

1. In a stockpot or Dutch oven, heat the oil over medium-high heat. Add the potatoes and onions and cook, stirring, until heated through.

2. Add the broth and Cajun seasoning and bring to a boil. Reduce the heat to medium-low, cover, and let the soup simmer for about 10 minutes, until the potatoes and onions are very tender. Stir in the milk and remove from the heat.

3. Using an immersion blender or countertop blender (be careful when blending hot soup!), puree the soup until smooth and thick. Add salt or more Cajun seasoning to taste. Reheat the soup over medium heat just until heated through.

4. Stir in the cheese until it melts and is incorporated.

5. Serve hot, with extra cheese sprinkled on top.

Optional Finishing Touch: Top your soup with minced scallions or chives and a dollop of sour cream.

Cooking Tip: Using a frozen mix of potatoes and onions cuts down on prep time significantly, but you could use 1½ cups chopped potatoes and ½ cup chopped onion in place of the frozen vegetables, if you have the fresh ingredients on hand.

Per serving: Calories: 556; Total Fat: 30g; Saturated Fat: 15g; Cholesterol: 72mg; Sodium: 603mg; Total Carbohydrates: 46g; Sugars: 8g; Protein: 26g

CHICKEN PASTA SOUP WITH PARMESAN

30 MINUTES OR LESS **ONE POT**

SERVES 2 / PREP TIME: 10 MINUTES / COOK TIME: 15 MINUTES

This delightful chicken soup is made even better with the addition of salty Parmesan cheese. It makes a perfect lunch on its own, or it can be paired with a salad or sandwich for a more substantial meal.

1 TABLESPOON OLIVE OIL

1 GARLIC CLOVE, MINCED

2 CUPS CHICKEN BROTH

½ TEASPOON KOSHER SALT

¼ TEASPOON FRESHLY
   GROUND BLACK PEPPER

4 OUNCES DITALINI PASTA

1 CUP SHREDDED
   COOKED CHICKEN

½ CUP GRATED PARMESAN
   CHEESE, PLUS
   ADDITIONAL FOR GARNISH

1. In a stockpot or Dutch oven, heat the oil over medium-high heat. Add the garlic and cook, stirring, for about 1 minute.

2. Add the broth, salt, and pepper and bring to a boil.

3. Reduce the heat to medium, stir in the pasta, and simmer for 8 to 10 minutes, until the pasta is tender.

4. Reduce the heat to medium-low and add the chicken. Simmer until the chicken is heated through.

5. Stir in the cheese until melted and incorporated.

6. Serve hot, with extra cheese sprinkled on top.

Optional Finishing Touch: Sprinkle chopped fresh flat-leaf parsley over the top as a garnish.

Pairing Tip: Thick slices of buttery garlic bread are delicious served alongside this soup.

Per serving: Calories: 493; Total Fat: 31g; Saturated Fat: 6g; Cholesterol: 99mg; Sodium: 729mg; Total Carbohydrates: 44g; Sugars: 2g; Protein: 41g

BLACK BEAN SOUP

30 MINUTES OR LESS **FREEZER-FRIENDLY** **ONE POT**

SERVES 2 / PREP TIME: 10 MINUTES / COOK TIME: 20 MINUTES

This Latin-inspired soup is proof that you don't need a lot of ingredients to make a flavorful dish—even one that is vegan! Add toppings to dress it up, give it some texture, and dial up the flavor.

1 TABLESPOON OLIVE OIL

½ ONION, DICED

1 (15-OUNCE) CAN BLACK BEANS, DRAINED AND RINSED, DIVIDED

2 CUPS VEGETABLE BROTH

1 CUP SALSA (MILD, MEDIUM, OR HOT)

2 TEASPOONS CHILI POWDER (PAGE 160) OR STORE-BOUGHT

KOSHER SALT (OPTIONAL)

1. In a stockpot or Dutch oven, heat the oil over medium-high heat. Add the onion and cook, stirring frequently, for about 5 minutes, until softened.

2. Add the beans, reserving ½ cup, the broth, salsa, and chili powder and bring to a boil. Reduce the heat to medium-low and simmer, stirring occasionally, for 10 minutes. Remove the pot from the heat.

3. Using an immersion blender or a countertop blender (be careful when blending hot soup!), puree the soup until smooth.

4. Return the soup to the heat and stir in the reserved ½ cup beans. Cook over medium heat for 5 more minutes, until heated through.

5. Add salt or other seasonings to taste. Serve hot.

Optional Finishing Touch: Garnish with shredded cheese, diced avocado, sour cream, diced pickled jalapeños, and chopped fresh cilantro.

Storage Tip: This soup freezes well. After cooking, let it cool to room temperature, then transfer it to a freezer-safe resealable plastic bag. Freeze it flat on a baking sheet. Store in the freezer for up to 3 months.

Per serving: Calories: 323; Total Fat: 10g; Saturated Fat: 2g; Cholesterol: 0mg; Sodium: 972mg; Total Carbohydrates: 44g; Sugars: 6g; Protein: 19g

CREAMY TOMATO SOUP

30 MINUTES OR LESS

SERVES 2 / PREP TIME: 10 MINUTES / COOK TIME: 10 MINUTES

On a rainy day, there's nothing better than a hot bowl of creamy tomato soup. This soup comes together easily in 20 minutes.

1 (28-OUNCE) CAN WHOLE TOMATOES (PREFERABLY SAN MARZANO)

2 TABLESPOONS OLIVE OIL

1 LARGE GARLIC CLOVE, MINCED

1 CUP VEGETABLE BROTH

3 TABLESPOONS HEAVY (WHIPPING) CREAM

2 TABLESPOONS CHOPPED FRESH BASIL, DIVIDED

KOSHER SALT

FRESHLY GROUND BLACK PEPPER

1. In a blender, puree the tomatoes and their juices and set aside.

2. In a stockpot or Dutch oven, heat the oil over medium heat. Add the garlic and cook, stirring, for 30 seconds, until fragrant.

3. Add the pureed tomatoes and broth and bring to a gentle boil. Reduce the heat to medium-low and simmer for 10 minutes.

4. Stir in the cream and 1 tablespoon of the basil. Season with salt and pepper.

5. Serve hot, garnished with the remaining 1 tablespoon basil.

Optional Finishing Touch: Sprinkle shredded Cheddar cheese or crumbled feta cheese over the hot soup just before serving.

Pairing Tip: Nothing goes better with a bowl of tomato soup than Grilled Cheese and Tomato Sandwiches with Olive Tapenade (page 50).

Per serving: Calories: 282; Total Fat: 23g; Saturated Fat: 8g; Cholesterol: 33mg; Sodium: 823mg; Total Carbohydrates: 18g; Sugars: 10g; Protein: 5g

PUMPKIN CURRY SOUP

30 MINUTES OR LESS   **FREEZER-FRIENDLY**   **ONE POT**

SERVES 2 / PREP TIME: 10 MINUTES / COOK TIME: 10 MINUTES

Curry pastes—both the Thai and Indian varieties—are among my favorite shortcut ingredients. Just a spoonful adds rich, complex, and layered flavor. This simple creamy pumpkin soup is a great example. Note that many commercial curry pastes contain shrimp or fish, so check the label carefully if you're cooking vegetarian.

1 TABLESPOON OLIVE OIL

1 TABLESPOON THAI RED CURRY PASTE

2 CUPS CHICKEN BROTH OR VEGETABLE BROTH

1 (15-OUNCE) CAN PUMPKIN PUREE

¾ CUP COCONUT MILK

2 TABLESPOONS CHOPPED FRESH CILANTRO

1. In a stockpot or Dutch oven, heat the oil over medium heat. Add the curry paste and cook, stirring, for 1 minute. Stir in the broth and pumpkin and bring to a boil.

2. Stir in the coconut milk and cook for 3 to 4 minutes, until the soup is very hot.

3. Serve hot, garnished with the cilantro.

Optional Finishing Touch: A squeeze of lime juice stirred into the soup just before serving adds brightness and is a nice balance to the spice of the curry paste.

Storage Tip: This soup freezes well. After cooking, let it cool to room temperature, then transfer it to a freezer-safe resealable plastic bag. Freeze it flat on a baking sheet. Store in the freezer for up to 3 months.

Per serving: Calories: 364; Total Fat: 43g; Saturated Fat: 19g; Cholesterol: 25mg; Sodium: 542mg; Total Carbohydrates: 21g; Sugars: 7g; Protein: 9g

BACON AND CORN CHOWDER

FREEZER-FRIENDLY **ONE POT**

SERVES 2 / PREP TIME: 5 MINUTES / COOK TIME: 30 MINUTES

Sweet corn and salty bacon are a delightful match. This soup gets body and flavor from corn, onion, garlic, and cream. Cooking the onion and garlic in the rendered bacon fat saves time, adds flavor, and means buying one less ingredient.

4 BACON SLICES, CHOPPED

½ ONION, DICED

1 GARLIC CLOVE, MINCED

2 CUPS FRESH OR FROZEN
  CORN KERNELS

2 CUPS WATER,
  CHICKEN BROTH, OR
  VEGETABLE BROTH

KOSHER SALT

FRESHLY GROUND
  BLACK PEPPER

½ CUP HEAVY
  (WHIPPING) CREAM

1. In a Dutch oven over medium-high heat, cook the bacon for about 6 minutes, until crisp. Transfer the bacon to a paper towel–lined plate.

2. Add the onion to the Dutch oven and cook in the bacon fat, stirring frequently, for about 5 minutes, until softened.

3. Stir in the garlic and cook, stirring, for 1 minute more.

4. Add the corn, water or broth, and salt and pepper to taste and bring to a boil.

5. Reduce the heat to medium-low and let simmer for about 15 minutes, until slightly thickened.

6. Using an immersion blender or a countertop blender (be careful when blending hot soup!), puree the soup until smooth.

7. Return the soup to the heat and stir in the cream. Warm over medium heat for about 3 minutes more, just until heated through.

8. Serve hot, with the bacon crumbled over the top.

Optional Finishing Touch: Top with shredded cheese, tortilla chips, sliced scallions, sour cream, or diced avocado.

Variation: Make this recipe vegetarian by using vegetarian bacon, olive oil rather than bacon fat, and vegetable broth.

Storage Tip: This soup freezes well. After cooking (and before stirring in the cream), let the soup cool to room temperature, then transfer it to a freezer-safe resealable plastic bag. Freeze it flat on a baking sheet. Store in the freezer for up to 3 months. To serve, thaw in the refrigerator overnight, then heat in a saucepan on the stovetop or in the microwave. Stir in the cream and crumble the bacon over the top just before serving.

Per serving: Calories: 504; Total Fat: 39g; Saturated Fat: 19g; Cholesterol: 123mg; Sodium: 1,289mg; Total Carbohydrates: 22g; Sugars: 5g; Protein: 18g

TACO CHICKEN SOUP

30 MINUTES OR LESS **FREEZER-FRIENDLY** **ONE POT**

SERVES 2 / PREP TIME: 5 MINUTES / COOK TIME: 15 MINUTES

When you don't have loads of free time to spend in the kitchen, rotisserie chicken from the market is your best friend. Buy a chicken on Monday and use it for meals throughout the workweek. This Mexican-inspired soup is quick and easy to make, and it has lots of flavor and body thanks to the refried beans and smoky fire-roasted tomatoes with green chile.

2 CUPS CHICKEN BROTH

1½ CUPS REFRIED BEANS

1½ CUPS CANNED
   FIRE-ROASTED DICED
   TOMATOES WITH
   GREEN CHILE

1 CUP SHREDDED
   COOKED CHICKEN

1 TABLESPOON CHILI
   POWDER (PAGE 160) OR
   STORE-BOUGHT

KOSHER SALT

FRESHLY GROUND
   BLACK PEPPER

1. In a stockpot or Dutch oven, combine the broth, beans, tomatoes and their juices, chicken, and chili powder and bring to a boil over medium-high heat.

2. Reduce the heat to low, cover, and simmer for 15 minutes.

3. Season with salt and pepper. Serve hot.

Optional Finishing Touch: Top with your favorite taco or chili toppings. Try shredded cheese, diced red onion, sliced scallions, sour cream, guacamole, or salsa.

Variation: If you prefer a spicier soup, use spicy refried beans with jalapeños or add hot sauce to taste.

Storage Tip: This soup freezes well. After cooking, let it cool to room temperature, then transfer it to a freezer-safe resealable plastic bag. Freeze it flat on a baking sheet. Store in the freezer for up to 3 months.

Per serving: Calories: 349; Total Fat: 20g; Saturated Fat: 2g; Cholesterol: 94mg; Sodium: 1,042mg; Total Carbohydrates: 35g; Sugars: 3g; Protein: 37g

WHITE CHICKEN CHILI

30 MINUTES OR LESS **FREEZER-FRIENDLY** **ONE POT**

SERVES 2 / PREP TIME: 5 MINUTES / COOK TIME: 10 MINUTES

White chicken chili is a light alternative to chili made with beef, pinto beans, and a red chile–infused sauce. This one is really more green than white because it's made from a combination of chicken broth and salsa verde. Chicken and white beans make it perfect for a healthy lunch or dinner.

2 CUPS CHICKEN BROTH

2 CUPS SALSA VERDE

1 (15-OUNCE) CAN WHITE
  BEANS, DRAINED
  AND RINSED

1 CUP SHREDDED
  COOKED CHICKEN

½ TEASPOON
  GROUND CUMIN

KOSHER SALT

FRESHLY GROUND
  BLACK PEPPER

1. In a stockpot or Dutch oven, combine the broth, salsa, beans, chicken, and cumin. Season to taste with salt and pepper. Bring to a boil over medium heat.

2. Reduce the heat to low and simmer, uncovered, for about 10 minutes, until bubbling and heated through. Serve hot.

Optional Finishing Touch: Top your chili with a dollop of sour cream and chopped fresh cilantro.

Storage Tip: This chili freezes well. After cooking, let it cool to room temperature, then transfer it to a freezer-safe resealable plastic bag. Freeze it flat on a baking sheet. Store in the freezer for up to 3 months.

Per serving: Calories: 394; Total Fat: 19g; Saturated Fat: 1g; Cholesterol: 79mg; Sodium: 1,630mg; Total Carbohydrates: 46g; Sugars: 4g; Protein: 40g

GRILLED PROSCIUTTO AND FIG SANDWICHES

30 MINUTES OR LESS   **FEELING FANCY**   **ONE PAN**

SERVES 2 / PREP TIME: 5 MINUTES / COOK TIME: 10 MINUTES

This simple sandwich combines salty, sweet, and savory into one gooey grilled cheese package. It makes a delightful lunch on its own, or serve it with a green salad with balsamic dressing on the side.

2 OUNCES THINLY SLICED
PROSCIUTTO

4 SOURDOUGH
BREAD SLICES

½ CUP SHREDDED
FONTINA CHEESE

½ CUP BABY ARUGULA

2 TABLESPOONS FIG JAM

2 TABLESPOONS OLIVE OIL

1. Divide the prosciutto slices evenly between two slices of the bread. Top the prosciutto with the cheese and arugula, dividing them equally. Spread the fig jam on the remaining two slices of bread. Place the jam-spread bread slices on top of the prosciutto, cheese, and arugula–topped halves.

2. In a large skillet, heat the oil over medium-high heat. Place the sandwiches in the pan, cover, and reduce the heat to medium. Cook for 3 to 4 minutes, until the bottom of the bread is golden brown. Flip the sandwiches over carefully, cover the pan again, and cook for another 3 to 4 minutes, until the second side is browned and crisp and the cheese is melted.

3. Remove the sandwiches from the pan. Cut each in half diagonally and serve immediately.

Variation: Substitute fruit preserves like strawberry or plum for the fig jam, or even try adding sliced fresh fruit, like figs, pears, or apples, in its place.

Per serving: Calories: 500; Total Fat: 25g; Saturated Fat: 8g; Cholesterol: 46mg; Sodium: 976mg; Total Carbohydrates: 48g; Sugars: 13g; Protein: 21g

CURRY CHICKEN SALAD SANDWICHES

30 MINUTES OR LESS

SERVES 2 / PREP TIME: 10 MINUTES

One of the best ways to use leftover roasted chicken (or a rotisserie chicken from the market) is to make chicken salad. This version is spiced with curry powder, which gives it layers of flavor. Apples add extra flavor contrast and texture.

10 OUNCES COOKED
  CHICKEN, DICED
3 TABLESPOONS
  MAYONNAISE
1 TABLESPOON
  CURRY POWDER
1 MEDIUM APPLE, PEELED,
  CORED, AND DICED
KOSHER SALT
FRESHLY GROUND
  BLACK PEPPER
4 SLICES SANDWICH BREAD

1. In a medium bowl, combine the chicken, mayonnaise, curry powder, and apple. Season with salt and pepper.

2. Cover and refrigerate for at least 30 minutes to let the flavors meld.

3. Spoon the mixture onto two slices of the bread. Top with the remaining slices of bread, and cut each sandwich in half diagonally. Serve immediately.

Optional Finishing Touch: Add lettuce for a fresh crunch with each bite.

Variation: Add diced celery, shredded carrots, or both for more texture and as a delicious way to sneak in some vegetables.

Per serving: Calories: 556; Total Fat: 22g; Saturated Fat: 4g; Cholesterol: 117mg; Sodium: 569mg; Total Carbohydrates: 40g; Sugars: 15g; Protein: 49g

CHICKEN CAESAR WRAP

30 MINUTES OR LESS

SERVES 2 / PREP TIME: 5 MINUTES

The combination of salty Parmesan cheese and lemony Caesar salad dressing adds pizzazz to this go-to lunch.

2 WHOLE-WHEAT WRAPS
  OR LARGE WHOLE-WHEAT
  FLOUR TORTILLAS
1 CUP CHOPPED
  ROMAINE LETTUCE
¾ CUP SHREDDED OR DICED
  COOKED CHICKEN
¼ CUP CAESAR SALAD
  DRESSING
3 TABLESPOONS GRATED
  PARMESAN CHEESE

1. On a clean work surface, lay the wraps out flat.

2. Top each wrap with half the lettuce and half the chicken. Drizzle the dressing and sprinkle the cheese over the filling on of each wrap, dividing evenly.

3. Fold the sides of each wrap over the filling, then roll up the wrap from the bottom to the top like a burrito. Slice each wrap in half and serve immediately.

Optional Finishing Touch: Add 2 or 3 anchovy fillets to each wrap for even more flavor.

Variation: To make a vegetarian version, use a vegetarian Caesar dressing and substitute canned chickpeas (drained and rinsed) for the chicken.

Per serving: Calories: 440; Total Fat: 25g; Saturated Fat: 6g; Cholesterol: 55mg; Sodium: 716mg; Total Carbohydrates: 27g; Sugars: 2g; Protein: 27g

BACON AND EGG SALAD SANDWICHES

30 MINUTES OR LESS

SERVES 2 / PREP TIME: 10 MINUTES / COOK TIME: 5 MINUTES

Bacon and eggs aren't just for breakfast anymore. This egg salad sandwich, studded with bacon and piled on a flaky croissant, is always a hit when served.

4 BACON SLICES

4 HARD-BOILED
   LARGE EGGS, PEELED
   AND CHOPPED

3 TABLESPOONS
   MAYONNAISE

1 DILL PICKLE, CHOPPED

KOSHER SALT

FRESHLY GROUND
   BLACK PEPPER

2 CROISSANTS, SPLIT

1. In a large skillet, cook the bacon over medium-high heat until crisp, about 5 minutes. Transfer to a paper towel–lined plate and let cool.

2. In a medium bowl, combine the eggs, mayonnaise, and pickle. Crumble the bacon into the mixture and stir gently to combine. Season to taste with salt and pepper.

3. Spoon the egg salad into the croissants and serve immediately.

Optional Finishing Touch: Top with a handful of baby arugula or sprinkle in some fresh chives for added flavor and a splash of color.

Pairing Tip: To balance the richness of this sandwich, serve with a fresh fruit salad on the side.

Per serving: Calories: 759; Total Fat: 55g; Saturated Fat: 18g; Cholesterol: 466mg; Sodium: 1,571mg; Total Carbohydrates: 33g; Sugars: 9g; Protein: 32g

GRILLED CHEESE AND TOMATO SANDWICHES WITH OLIVE TAPENADE

30 MINUTES OR LESS   **ONE PAN**

SERVES 2 / PREP TIME: 5 MINUTES / COOK TIME: 10 MINUTES

Olive tapenade is full of umami and lends deep, savory flavor to this simple grilled cheese sandwich. Melted mozzarella is the perfect creamy binder, bringing together the salty tapenade with the fresh flavors of tomato and arugula.

¼ CUP OLIVE TAPENADE (STORE-BOUGHT)

4 SOURDOUGH BREAD SLICES

4 THICK SLICES FRESH MOZZARELLA

1 LARGE TOMATO, SLICED

1 CUP ARUGULA

3 TABLESPOONS OLIVE OIL OR BUTTER, AT ROOM TEMPERATURE, DIVIDED

1. Spread the tapenade on two slices of the bread.

2. Layer the mozzarella and tomato slices on top of the tapenade.

3. Top with the arugula and the remaining slices of bread.

4. Brush the outsides of the bread generously with oil.

5. In a large nonstick skillet, heat the remaining oil over medium-high heat.

6. Cook the sandwiches for 3 to 4 minutes per side, until the bottom of the bread is golden brown and crisp. Flip the sandwiches over carefully and cook until the second side is golden brown and the cheese is melted.

7. Slice each sandwich in half diagonally and serve immediately.

Cooking Tip: Grill this sandwich a little longer for meltier cheese and crispier bread.

Per serving: Calories: 604; Total Fat: 39g; Saturated Fat: 4g; Cholesterol: 40mg; Sodium: 863mg; Total Carbohydrates: 44g; Sugars: 4g; Protein: 19g

PESTO CHICKPEA SALAD SANDWICHES

30 MINUTES OR LESS

SERVES 2 / PREP TIME: 5 MINUTES

Chickpeas are a great alternative to chicken or tuna. Prepared pesto acts as a flavorful dressing and really brings the ingredients together, so you don't need to add much else to make this sandwich delicious.

1 (15-OUNCE) CAN
   CHICKPEAS, DRAINED
   AND RINSED
¼ CUP HERB PESTO
   (PAGE 163) OR
   STORE-BOUGHT
JUICE OF ½ LEMON
KOSHER SALT
FRESHLY GROUND
   BLACK PEPPER
4 WHOLE-WHEAT
   SANDWICH BREAD SLICES
1 CUP ARUGULA
   OR CHOPPED
   ROMAINE LETTUCE

1. In a small bowl, combine the chickpeas, pesto, and lemon juice and, using a fork, stir to mix while mashing some of the chickpeas. Season with salt and pepper.

2. Spoon the mixture onto two slices of the bread. Top with the arugula and the remaining slices of bread. Cut each sandwich in half diagonally and serve immediately.

Optional Finishing Touch: Stir sliced or chopped marinated sun-dried tomatoes into the chickpea salad for an even tangier flavor.

Cooking Tip: Toast the bread before assembling the sandwich for a bit more crunch.

Per serving: Calories: 483; Total Fat: 18g; Saturated Fat: 4g; Cholesterol: 8mg; Sodium: 548mg; Total Carbohydrates: 60g; Sugars: 12g; Protein: 22g

*Watermelon and
Feta Salad, page 60*

Chapter Four

SALADS

PESTO PASTA SALAD

30 MINUTES OR LESS

SERVES 2 / PREP TIME: 5 MINUTES / COOK TIME: 10 MINUTES

Pasta salad makes a delicious take-along lunch or a quick light dinner, especially on a warm summer day when something cool is in order. The green olives in this salad add umami.

4 OUNCES FUSILLI OR
ROTELLE PASTA

1 CUP HALVED CHERRY
TOMATOES

¼ CUP HERB PESTO
(PAGE 163) OR
STORE-BOUGHT

1 TABLESPOON CHOPPED
GREEN OLIVES

1 TABLESPOON OLIVE OIL

¼ CUP GRATED
PARMESAN CHEESE

KOSHER SALT

FRESHLY GROUND
BLACK PEPPER

1. Bring a pot of water to a boil and cook the pasta according to the package directions until al dente. Drain and rinse with cold water to cool quickly.

2. In a medium bowl, toss the pasta, tomatoes, pesto, olives, and oil. Add the cheese and toss to incorporate. Season with salt and pepper. Serve at room temperature.

Variation: You can dress up this simple salad by adding any green vegetables you like. I like to add fresh or thawed frozen peas and thinly sliced fresh basil.

Per serving: Calories: 462; Total Fat: 24g; Saturated Fat: 6g; Cholesterol: 18mg; Sodium: 469mg; Total Carbohydrates: 49g; Sugars: 6g; Protein: 16g

PANZANELLA

30 MINUTES OR LESS **FEELING FANCY**

SERVES 2 / PREP TIME: 5 MINUTES, PLUS 20 MINUTES TO CHILL

Panzanella is an Italian bread salad that combines day-old bread with fresh, juicy tomatoes. The juice from the tomatoes and the dressing soak into the bread so that each bite is packed with flavor. It's hearty and refreshing at the same time.

2 CUPS CUBED DAY-OLD
   BAGUETTE OR RUSTIC
   ITALIAN BREAD

2 LARGE RIPE TOMATOES,
   CUT INTO 1-INCH CUBES

1 PERSIAN
   CUCUMBER, CHOPPED

¼ CUP CHOPPED
   FRESH BASIL

⅓ CUP SIMPLE VINAIGRETTE
   DRESSING (PAGE 164) OR
   STORE-BOUGHT

KOSHER SALT

FRESHLY GROUND
   BLACK PEPPER

1. In a medium bowl, toss together the bread, tomatoes, cucumber, and basil. Add the dressing and toss to mix well. Season with salt and pepper.

2. Refrigerate for 15 to 20 minutes to allow the dressing to soak into the bread and the flavors to meld. Serve chilled or at room temperature.

Variation: While this simple salad packs plenty of flavor on its own, you can mix in halved Kalamata olives, diced red onion or bell peppers, and crumbled feta cheese, if you want to try something different.

Per serving: Calories: 217; Total Fat: 8g; Saturated Fat: 0g; Cholesterol: 0mg; Sodium: 587mg; Total Carbohydrates: 32g; Sugars: 12g; Protein: 5g

SPANISH-STYLE CHICKPEA AND OLIVE SALAD

30 MINUTES OR LESS **FEELING FANCY**

SERVES 2 / PREP TIME: 5 MINUTES

This easy salad is a take on a classic Spanish tapas dish. It gets an air of sophistication from sherry vinegar, green olives, and Manchego cheese. Serve it as a side or make a meal of it.

1 (15-OUNCE) CAN
  CHICKPEAS, DRAINED
  AND RINSED
2 CELERY STALKS, CHOPPED
¼ CUP CHOPPED
  GREEN OLIVES
¼ CUP OLIVE OIL
2 TABLESPOONS
  SHERRY VINEGAR
KOSHER SALT
FRESHLY GROUND
  BLACK PEPPER
¼ CUP GRATED
  MANCHEGO CHEESE

1. In a large bowl, toss together the chickpeas, celery, and olives.

2. Add the oil and vinegar and toss to combine. Season with salt and pepper.

3. Top with the cheese and serve.

Flavor Tip: You can boost the flavor in this dish by adding 1 minced garlic clove, 1 tablespoon chopped fresh flat-leaf parsley, ½ cup diced cured Spanish chorizo, and ½ cup diced roasted piquillo peppers.

Per serving: Calories: 535; Total Fat: 38g; Saturated Fat: 8g; Cholesterol: 15mg; Sodium: 649mg; Total Carbohydrates: 40g; Sugars: 6g; Protein: 15g

CRUNCHY APPLE AND CABBAGE SLAW

30 MINUTES OR LESS

SERVES 2 / PREP TIME: 5 MINUTES

This quick slaw makes a great side dish for burgers or grilled meats or fish. It is especially delicious on a pulled pork sandwich. Choose a tart green apple like Granny Smith for this slaw.

⅓ CUP MAYONNAISE

1½ TABLESPOONS APPLE
   CIDER VINEGAR

1½ TABLESPOONS SUGAR

2 CUPS SHREDDED
   CABBAGE

1 SMALL APPLE, CORED
   AND CUT INTO
   MATCHSTICK-SIZE PIECES

KOSHER SALT

FRESHLY GROUND
   BLACK PEPPER

1. In a medium bowl, mix together the mayonnaise, vinegar, and sugar.

2. Add the cabbage and apple and toss to coat well. Season with salt and pepper.

3. Serve immediately or refrigerate for up to 2 days.

Optional Finishing Touch: Add toasted pumpkin seeds, dried cranberries, or both for even more flavor and textural contrast.

Per serving: Calories: 338; Total Fat: 25g; Saturated Fat: 4g; Cholesterol: 13mg; Sodium: 317mg; Total Carbohydrates: 29g; Sugars: 23g; Protein: 1g

BISTRO SALAD

30 MINUTES OR LESS   **FEELING FANCY**

SERVES 2 / PREP TIME: 5 MINUTES / COOK TIME: 10 MINUTES

To make this salad even more reminiscent of the ones you find in French bistros, look for a mixed-greens blend that includes frisée, a bitter green that is also known as curly endive or chicory. The leaves are very curly and nicely hold the salad's eggs, which should be somewhere between soft-boiled and hard-boiled.

2 LARGE EGGS

2 CUPS MIXED
 SALAD GREENS

¼ CUP SIMPLE VINAIGRETTE
 DRESSING (PAGE 164) OR
 STORE-BOUGHT

2 TABLESPOONS CRUMBLED
 BLUE CHEESE

2 BACON SLICES, COOKED
 UNTIL CRISP AND THEN
 CRUMBLED

1. Fill a medium saucepan with water and bring to a boil. Gently add the eggs and reduce the heat to medium. Cook the eggs for 10 minutes, then remove the pan from the heat. Drain the eggs and immediately run cold water over them. Transfer the eggs to a bowl filled with ice water.

2. In a medium bowl, toss together the greens and dressing. Divide the greens between two individual serving bowls. Sprinkle blue cheese and bacon over the top of each dish.

3. Carefully crack and peel the eggs, and place an egg on top of each salad. Serve immediately.

Optional Finishing Touch: Add Spicy Candied Pecans (page 153), diced pear or apple, or dried cranberries for added flavor and crunch.

Pairing Tip: This salad goes great with a piece of crusty sourdough bread served on the side.

Per serving: Calories: 245; Total Fat: 15g; Saturated Fat: 6g; Cholesterol: 213mg; Sodium: 875mg; Total Carbohydrates: 11g; Sugars: 7g; Protein: 16g

GINGER MISO CHICKEN SALAD

30 MINUTES OR LESS

SERVES 2 / PREP TIME: 5 MINUTES

If you've got leftover cooked chicken and ginger miso dressing either already made or in a bottle from the supermarket, this recipe can be on the table in five minutes. It's not cheating to use a store-bought dressing you like—I like the Red Shell brands, including their Japanese miso dressings. You can also use the variation of the Simple Vinaigrette Dressing (page 164) to make your own.

2 CUPS CHOPPED ROMAINE LETTUCE

1 CUP SHREDDED COOKED CHICKEN

¼ CUP COOKED SHELLED EDAMAME

1 MEDIUM CARROT, SHREDDED

¼ CUP SIMPLE VINAIGRETTE WITH GINGER MISO (PAGE 164) OR STORE-BOUGHT

In a large bowl, toss together the lettuce, chicken, edamame, and carrot. Add the dressing and toss to coat. Serve immediately.

Finishing Touch: Garnish with thinly sliced cucumber or celery, toasted sesame seeds, or sliced snow peas.

Pairing Tip: Serve with a side of cooked spaghetti or soba noodles tossed with a bit of toasted sesame oil.

Per serving: Calories: 214; Total Fat: 10g; Saturated Fat: 1g; Cholesterol: 54mg; Sodium: 92mg; Total Carbohydrates: 7g; Sugars: 2g; Protein: 23g

WATERMELON AND FETA SALAD

30 MINUTES OR LESS

SERVES 2 / PREP TIME: 5 MINUTES

This salad combines a refreshing fruit with salty feta cheese, Kalamata olives, and tart red wine vinegar. Beware: This salad is addictive.

2 CUPS CUBED
  WATERMELON

1 CUP DICED CUCUMBER

¼ CUP CRUMBLED
  FETA CHEESE

¼ CUP HALVED
  KALAMATA OLIVES

2 TABLESPOONS RED
  WINE VINEGAR

2 TABLESPOONS OLIVE OIL

KOSHER SALT

FRESHLY GROUND
  BLACK PEPPER

1. In a large bowl, combine the watermelon, cucumber, cheese, and olives and toss gently to combine.

2. In a small bowl, whisk together the vinegar and oil and season with a pinch each of salt and pepper.

3. Add the dressing to the salad and gently toss. Taste and season with more salt and pepper, if needed. Serve immediately.

Optional Finishing Touch: Sprinkle 2 tablespoons chopped fresh mint over the top.

Variation: Use lime juice in place of red wine vinegar for a slightly different flavor.

Per serving: Calories: 326; Total Fat: 26g; Saturated Fat: 6g; Cholesterol: 17mg; Sodium: 1,021mg; Total Carbohydrates: 19g; Sugars: 11g; Protein: 9g

MIXED GREENS WITH PEARS AND BLUE CHEESE

30 MINUTES OR LESS

SERVES 2 / PREP TIME: 5 MINUTES

This is my go-to fall or winter salad. Bitter greens, sweet pear, candied nuts, rich blue cheese, and a creamy tart dressing make it totally crave-worthy. It's great as a side or main dish.

3 CUPS MIXED GREENS

1 LARGE PEAR, CORED AND DICED

¼ CUP SIMPLE VINAIGRETTE DRESSING (PAGE 164) OR STORE-BOUGHT

¼ CUP CRUMBLED BLUE CHEESE

2 TABLESPOONS CHOPPED SPICY CANDIED PECANS (PAGE 153)

1. In a large bowl, combine the greens and pear and toss gently.

2. Top with the dressing and toss to coat.

3. Sprinkle the cheese and pecans over the top. Serve immediately.

Variation: Use crumbled goat cheese in place of the blue cheese and a store-bought balsamic vinaigrette in place of the dressing, and you've got a whole different salad.

Per serving: Calories: 310; Total Fat: 23g; Saturated Fat: 5g; Cholesterol: 13mg; Sodium: 644mg; Total Carbohydrates: 21g; Sugars: 11g; Protein: 7g

LEMONY BRUSSELS SPROUT SLAW

30 MINUTES OR LESS

SERVES 2 / PREP TIME: 5 MINUTES

Brussels sprouts make a great alternative to cabbage slaw. They're sturdy like cabbage and have a bitter flavor that pairs wonderfully with the tartness of lemon juice. This slaw makes a refreshing side dish, especially for grilled meats. Add some white beans or chickpeas to turn the salad into a whole meal.

¼ CUP OLIVE OIL

1½ TABLESPOONS FRESHLY
   SQUEEZED LEMON JUICE

KOSHER SALT

FRESHLY GROUND
   BLACK PEPPER

8 OUNCES BRUSSELS
   SPROUTS, SHREDDED
   OR THINLY SLICED

¼ CUP SLIVERED
   ALMONDS, TOASTED

¼ CUP FRESHLY GRATED
   PARMESAN CHEESE

1. In a medium bowl, whisk together the oil and lemon juice. Season with salt and pepper.

2. Add the Brussels sprouts and almonds and toss to coat.

3. Serve immediately, or cover and refrigerate for an hour to allow the flavors to meld and the sprouts to soften.

4. Just before serving, toss with the cheese.

Optional Finishing Touch: For some herby flavor, sprinkle chopped fresh thyme, sage, or oregano over the top.

Variation: Add diced apples to the salad for more texture and added flavor.

Per serving: Calories: 381; Total Fat: 35g; Saturated Fat: 6g; Cholesterol: 10mg; Sodium: 238mg; Total Carbohydrates: 14g; Sugars: 3g; Protein: 11g

LENTIL SALAD WITH CHERRY TOMATOES AND GOAT CHEESE

30 MINUTES OR LESS

SERVES 2 / PREP TIME: 5 MINUTES

Lentils are nutritious and super easy to cook. This lentil salad can be a hearty side or a satisfying light meal. The lentils are a great foil for the bright flavors of the vinegar, fresh tomatoes, basil, and goat cheese.

3 TABLESPOONS OLIVE OIL

2 TABLESPOONS WHITE
WINE VINEGAR

KOSHER SALT

FRESHLY GROUND
BLACK PEPPER

1 CUP COOKED LENTILS

1 CUP HALVED CHERRY
TOMATOES

¼ CUP CRUMBLED
GOAT CHEESE

1 TABLESPOON MINCED
FRESH BASIL

1. In a large bowl, whisk together the oil and vinegar. Season with salt and pepper.

2. Add the lentils and tomatoes and toss to coat.

3. Serve immediately, or cover and refrigerate for about an hour to let the flavors meld.

4. Just before serving, sprinkle the cheese and basil over the top.

Optional Finishing Touch: Add sliced fresh chives or scallions for extra flavor or add 1 tablespoon Dijon mustard to the dressing. If you're not cooking for a vegetarian, you could add a couple slices of crumbled cooked bacon.

Cooking Tip: Canned lentils are available in many supermarkets, and you can find cooked lentils in the refrigerator section.

Per serving: Calories: 355; Total Fat: 24g; Saturated Fat: 5g; Cholesterol: 10mg; Sodium: 142mg; Total Carbohydrates: 24g; Sugars: 4g; Protein: 12g

Sweet Potato Noodles with Sage Brown Butter, page 68

Chapter Five

VEGETARIAN ENTRÉES

ZOODLE BOWLS WITH CHERRY TOMATOES AND RICOTTA

30 MINUTES OR LESS   **ONE PAN**

SERVES 2 / PREP TIME: 5 MINUTES / COOK TIME: 15 MINUTES

When you want a quick bowl of pasta but are limiting your carbs, zoodles (zucchini noodles) are just the thing. Top them with garlicky blistered cherry tomatoes and creamy ricotta cheese and you'll be in heaven.

3 TEASPOONS OLIVE
  OIL, DIVIDED, PLUS
  ADDITIONAL FOR GARNISH
1½ CUPS CHERRY TOMATOES
1 GARLIC CLOVE, MINCED
2 ZUCCHINI, SPIRALIZED
KOSHER SALT
FRESHLY GROUND
  BLACK PEPPER
½ CUP WHOLE-MILK
  RICOTTA CHEESE

1. In a skillet, heat 1½ teaspoons of the oil over medium heat. Add the tomatoes and cook, stirring occasionally, until the tomatoes soften and begin to burst, about 10 minutes. Stir in the garlic and cook for about 30 seconds more. Transfer the tomatoes to a bowl and wipe out the pan.

2. In the same skillet, heat the remaining 1½ teaspoons oil. Add the zucchini and season with salt and pepper. Cook, tossing occasionally, for 5 to 7 minutes, until the zucchini is tender.

3. To serve, divide the zucchini between two individual serving bowls. Top each with half the tomatoes and half the ricotta. Garnish with a drizzle of oil, a pinch of salt, and a bit of pepper.

Optional Finishing Touch: Garnish with 2 tablespoons chopped fresh basil, oregano, or mint and a pinch of red pepper flakes, as you like.

Pairing Tip: Serve this dish alongside a simple roast chicken or Cider and Dijon Roasted Pork (page 135).

Per serving: Calories: 172; Total Fat: 12g; Saturated Fat: 4g; Cholesterol: 16mg; Sodium: 130mg; Total Carbohydrates: 13g; Sugars: 7g; Protein: 7g

SWEET POTATO AND BLACK BEAN TACOS

SERVES 2 / PREP TIME: 5 MINUTES / COOK TIME: 45 MINUTES

These vegetarian tacos can also be dressed up with any number of delicious toppings.

1 POUND SWEET POTATOES, PEELED AND CUT INTO 1-INCH CUBES

1 TABLESPOON OLIVE OIL

KOSHER SALT

FRESHLY GROUND BLACK PEPPER

1 CUP COOKED OR CANNED BLACK BEANS

1 TABLESPOON CHILI POWDER (PAGE 160) OR STORE-BOUGHT

4 CORN TORTILLAS

1 TABLESPOON CHOPPED FRESH CILANTRO

1. Preheat the oven to 425°F. Line a baking sheet with parchment paper or aluminum foil.

2. Toss the sweet potatoes with the oil, and season generously with salt and pepper. Arrange in a single layer on the prepared baking sheet and bake for 35 to 40 minutes, tossing once or twice, until tender and beginning to brown.

3. In a small saucepan, combine the beans with the chili powder and heat over medium heat for about 4 minutes.

4. Warm the tortillas either wrapped in foil in the oven or over the flame of a gas burner.

5. Divide the tortillas between two serving plates, then divide the sweet potatoes evenly between them. Top with the beans. Garnish with the cilantro and serve immediately.

Optional Finishing Touch: Garnish with diced avocado or guacamole, diced red onion, a squeeze of fresh lime juice, and crumbled or shredded cotija, feta, or Cheddar cheese.

Pairing Tip: Serve with Fresh Salsa Picante (page 162).

Per serving: Calories: 485; Total Fat: 10g; Saturated Fat: 2g; Cholesterol: 0mg; Sodium: 263mg; Total Carbohydrates: 89g; Sugars: 19g; Protein: 14g

SWEET POTATO NOODLES WITH SAGE BROWN BUTTER

30 MINUTES OR LESS **ONE PAN**

SERVES 2 / PREP TIME: 5 MINUTES / COOK TIME: 15 MINUTES

Spiralized sweet potatoes make a perfect grain-free substitute for pasta. You will love the natural sweetness they bring to this dish. Brown butter and sage is a classic flavor combination.

3 TABLESPOONS
   UNSALTED BUTTER

¼ CUP PACKED FRESH
   SAGE LEAVES

2 MEDIUM SWEET
   POTATOES, PEELED AND
   SPIRALIZED

KOSHER SALT

FRESHLY GROUND
   BLACK PEPPER

PINCH GROUND NUTMEG

¼ CUP FRESHLY GRATED
   PARMESAN CHEESE

1. In a large skillet, melt the butter over medium heat. Continue to cook until it foams and then the foam subsides. Add the sage and cook until the butter begins to brown and the leaves start to crisp, about 5 minutes. Keep your eye on the pan because the butter can burn quickly.

2. Add the sweet potato noodles and cook, stirring frequently, for 5 to 7 minutes, until tender. Season with salt, pepper, and the nutmeg.

3. Divide the noodles between two individual serving plates, sprinkle with the cheese, and serve immediately.

Optional Finishing Touch: For a bit of crunch, sprinkle 1 to 2 tablespoons chopped toasted walnuts, pecans, or hazelnuts over the top.

Variation: This sage brown butter sauce goes equally well with al dente spaghetti if you don't have sweet potato or a spiralizer on hand.

Pairing Tip: For a hearty meal, serve this dish alongside Italian-style meatballs or Mushroom and Lentil Meatballs (page 78).

Per serving: Calories: 310; Total Fat: 20g; Saturated Fat: 13g; Cholesterol: 56mg; Sodium: 402mg; Total Carbohydrates: 27g; Sugars: 6g; Protein: 7g

CRISPY CHICKPEAS WITH SPINACH AND FRIED EGGS

30 MINUTES OR LESS

SERVES 2 / PREP TIME: 5 MINUTES / COOK TIME: 15 MINUTES

Chickpeas are a great ingredient to add to vegetable stews and salads for a bit of extra protein. Chickpeas are also affordable and versatile, and this dish is a perfect example of their many uses.

2 TABLESPOONS OLIVE
   OIL, DIVIDED
1 (15-OUNCE) CAN
   CHICKPEAS, DRAINED
   AND RINSED
½ TEASPOON
   SMOKED PAPRIKA
KOSHER SALT
2 LARGE EGGS
2 CUPS FRESH
   BABY SPINACH
FRESHLY GROUND
   BLACK PEPPER
½ LEMON

1. In a medium skillet, heat 1 tablespoon of the oil over medium heat. Add the chickpeas, paprika, and a pinch of salt and stir to combine. Cook, stirring occasionally, for about 10 minutes, until the chickpeas are lightly browned.

2. Meanwhile, in another medium skillet, heat the remaining 1 tablespoon oil over medium-high heat. Crack the eggs into the pan and fry for about 5 minutes, until the whites are set but the yolks are still runny, reducing the heat as needed to prevent the bottom of the eggs from burning.

3. Add the spinach to the chickpeas and cook, stirring, until it wilts. Season with salt and pepper.

4. To serve, divide the chickpeas between two individual serving bowls. Top each dish with an egg and squeeze a bit of lemon juice over the top. Serve immediately.

→

Optional Finishing Touch: This dish could easily hold up to a sprinkle of crisp cooked bacon, either vegetarian or not. A sprinkling of crumbled feta or grated Parmesan cheese would also be divine.

Pairing Tip: Serve with thick slices of buttered toasted sourdough bread.

Per serving: Calories: 406; Total Fat: 22g; Saturated Fat: 4g; Cholesterol: 186mg; Sodium: 180mg; Total Carbohydrates: 37g; Sugars: 7g; Protein: 18g

BUTTERNUT SQUASH
MAC 'N' CHEESE

30 MINUTES OR LESS

SERVES 2 / PREP TIME: 5 MINUTES / COOK TIME: 15 MINUTES

Mac 'n' cheese from a box is a popular go-to when there's no time to cook, but this recipe really doesn't take much more effort or time and puts the boxed stuff to shame. Plus, it has nutritious butternut squash hidden in the cheesy sauce.

8 OUNCES SMALL PASTA
   SHAPES (SHELLS
   OR ELBOWS)

1 TABLESPOON OLIVE OIL

8 OUNCES DICED PEELED
   BUTTERNUT SQUASH
   (ABOUT 2 CUPS)

¾ CUP VEGETABLE BROTH

1 CUP WHOLE MILK

1½ CUPS SHREDDED SHARP
   CHEDDAR CHEESE

KOSHER SALT

FRESHLY GROUND
   BLACK PEPPER

1. Bring a large pot of water to a boil and cook the pasta according to the package directions until al dente. Drain, reserving 1 cup of the cooking water, and set aside.

2. In a medium saucepan, heat the oil over medium-high heat. Add the squash and cook, stirring, for about 5 minutes, until it begins to brown.

3. Add the broth and bring to a simmer. Reduce the heat to medium-low, cover the saucepan, and cook, stirring occasionally, for about 10 minutes, until the squash is tender.

4. Transfer the squash to a blender, add the milk, and puree the mixture until smooth. (Be careful when blending hot liquids! If you can, leave the lid slightly open to vent steam, and puree in two batches, if necessary, to keep from overfilling the blender.)

5. Transfer the pureed mixture to the saucepan and heat over medium-high heat. Add the cheese and stir until it is completely melted and incorporated. Season with salt and pepper.

→

6. Pour the sauce over the pasta (either in the pasta cooking pot or in a serving bowl) and toss to mix. Add the reserved pasta cooking water if needed to thin the sauce. Serve hot.

Cooking Tip: Here's an extra cooking step that packs in tons of additional flavor, if you have the time or inclination. Transfer the mac 'n' cheese to an 8-inch square baking dish and spread it out in an even layer. Toss ½ cup panko bread crumbs with 1 tablespoon melted butter and sprinkle the mixture evenly over the mac 'n' cheese. Heat under the broiler for 2 to 3 minutes, until the bread crumbs are golden brown and crisp.

Per serving: Calories: 939; Total Fat: 43g; Saturated Fat: 21g; Cholesterol: 101mg; Sodium: 871mg; Total Carbohydrates: 95g; Sugars: 14g; Protein: 45g

CHEESY POLENTA BAKE

ONE PAN

SERVES 2 / PREP TIME: 5 MINUTES / COOK TIME: 1 HOUR

Polenta is often served as a side dish, but this easy casserole proves it can stand on its own. Baking polenta gives you the same creamy result as cooking it on the stovetop, but with none of the hands-on effort. You can top this dish with pasta sauce or roasted or sautéed vegetables.

OLIVE OIL OR OLIVE
  OIL SPRAY, FOR
  PREPARING THE PAN
1 CUP POLENTA
1 CUP HALF-AND-HALF
2 LARGE EGGS, BEATEN
¾ TEASPOON KOSHER SALT
1½ CUPS SHREDDED
  SHARP WHITE CHEDDAR
  CHEESE, DIVIDED

1. Preheat the oven to 350°F. Brush or spray an 8-inch square baking dish with oil.

2. In the baking dish, combine 4 cups water, the polenta, half-and-half, eggs, and salt and stir to mix well. Bake for 50 minutes.

3. Remove the baking dish from the oven, leaving the oven on, and stir in 1 cup of the cheese. Sprinkle the remaining ½ cup cheese over the top.

4. Return to the oven and bake for 10 minutes more. Serve hot.

Variation: You can mix any number of ingredients into the polenta before baking to add flavor and texture. Try adding 1 cup fresh or frozen corn kernels, diced roasted green chiles, diced marinated sun-dried tomatoes, or diced artichoke hearts.

Per serving: Calories: 657; Total Fat: 49g; Saturated Fat: 28g; Cholesterol: 319mg; Sodium: 1,113mg; Total Carbohydrates: 23g; Sugars: 1g; Protein: 32g

STIR-FRIED TOFU AND GREEN BEANS WITH GINGER

ONE PAN

**SERVES 2 / PREP TIME: 5 MINUTES, PLUS 15 MINUTES
TO PRESS THE TOFU / COOK TIME: 20 MINUTES**

The trick to delicious stir-fried tofu is to press the extra water out before cooking. This task takes a little time, but it's worth it. Without the excess water, the tofu really absorbs the other flavors in the dish.

½ (17-OUNCE) PACKAGE
  FIRM TOFU, CUT INTO
  1-INCH-THICK SLICES

2 TABLESPOONS
  VEGETABLE OIL, DIVIDED

1½ CUPS CHOPPED
  GREEN BEANS

2 TABLESPOONS
  LOW-SODIUM SOY SAUCE

2 TEASPOONS
  BROWN SUGAR

2 TEASPOONS GRATED
  FRESH GINGER

1. Preheat the oven to 400°F.

2. Lay a clean dish towel flat on a cutting board or countertop. Arrange the sliced tofu on top in a single layer. Cover with a second clean dish towel and place a baking sheet on top. Place something heavy like a cast-iron pan or Dutch oven on top and let stand for 15 minutes to press out the excess water. Cut the pressed tofu into 1-inch cubes.

3. In a large skillet, heat 1 tablespoon of the oil over medium-high heat. Add the tofu and cook, turning the slices occasionally, for 8 to 10 minutes, until golden brown. Transfer the tofu to a bowl or plate.

4. In the same skillet, heat the remaining 1 tablespoon oil over medium-high heat. Add the green beans and cook, stirring occasionally, for about 5 minutes, until tender.

5. Add the soy sauce, sugar, and ginger to the skillet and stir. Cook until the sauce begins to bubble and thicken, about 2 minutes more, then return the tofu to the pan.

6. Cook for about 3 minutes more, until the sauce coats the beans and tofu. Serve hot.

Variation: This recipe works with a variety of other vegetables as well, either replacing some of the green beans or in addition to them. I like diced carrots, red bell peppers, or sliced shiitake mushrooms.

Cooking Tip: For a thicker sauce, whisk 1 tablespoon cornstarch with 1 tablespoon water and add it to the pan after the soy sauce mixture starts to bubble.

Per serving: Calories: 247; Total Fat: 19g; Saturated Fat: 4g; Cholesterol: 0mg; Sodium: 800mg; Total Carbohydrates: 12g; Sugars: 6g; Protein: 12g

TOFU FRITTERS

**SERVES 2 / PREP TIME: 5 MINUTES, PLUS 25 MINUTES TO PRESS AND
MARINATE THE TOFU / COOK TIME: 10 MINUTES**

Try these fritters with steamed or sautéed vegetables and a dipping sauce like peanut sauce. Alternatively, serve them with steamed rice or noodles.

½ (17-OUNCE) PACKAGE
   FIRM TOFU, CUT INTO
   1-INCH-THICK SLICES

1 TABLESPOON SOY SAUCE

½ TEASPOON TOASTED
   SESAME OIL

1 SMALL GARLIC
   CLOVE, MINCED

PINCH KOSHER SALT

½ CUP CORNSTARCH

VEGETABLE OIL,
   FOR FRYING

1. Lay a clean dish towel out flat on a cutting board or countertop. Arrange the sliced tofu on top in a single layer. Cover with a second clean dish towel and place a baking sheet on top. Place something heavy like a cast-iron pan or Dutch oven on top and let stand for 15 minutes to press out the excess water. Cut the pressed tofu into 1-inch cubes.

2. In a medium bowl, combine the soy sauce, sesame oil, garlic, and salt. Add the tofu cubes and toss to coat. Let stand for 10 to 15 minutes.

3. Fill a saucepan with about 1 inch of vegetable oil and heat over medium-high heat until the oil shimmers.

4. Place the cornstarch in a small bowl, remove the tofu from the marinade, and dredge each piece in the cornstarch.

5. Working in batches, carefully lower the coated tofu cubes into the hot oil and cook, turning once, until golden brown, about 3 minutes. Drain the fritters on a paper towel–lined plate. Serve hot.

Pairing Tip: These fritters go great with peanut sauce. You can make your own quick peanut dipping sauce by combining ¼ cup creamy peanut butter with 2 tablespoons hoisin sauce and 1 teaspoon chili paste.

Per serving: Calories: 408; Total Fat: 27g; Saturated Fat: 3g; Cholesterol: 0mg; Sodium: 546mg; Total Carbohydrates: 32g; Sugars: 1g; Protein: 11g

MUSHROOM AND LENTIL MEATBALLS

SERVES 2 / PREP TIME: 10 MINUTES / COOK TIME: 45 MINUTES

These vegetarian meatballs make a filling meal on their own with a side salad or veggie. The lentils are quickly cooked, then blended with a mix of umami-rich mushrooms, garlic, and seasonings.

½ CUP DRIED
   BROWN LENTILS

4 OUNCES BUTTON
   OR CREMINI
   MUSHROOMS, SLICED

2 SMALL GARLIC
   CLOVES, MINCED

1 TEASPOON ITALIAN
   SEASONING

½ TEASPOON KOSHER SALT

¼ TEASPOON FRESHLY
   GROUND BLACK PEPPER

2 LARGE EGGS, BEATEN

2 TABLESPOONS OLIVE OIL

1. Preheat the oven to 400°F. Line a baking sheet with parchment paper.

2. In a small saucepan, combine 1 cup water and the lentils and bring to a boil. Reduce the heat to low and cook for 10 minutes. Drain the lentils and let them cool for several minutes.

3. Transfer the lentils to a food processor and add the mushrooms, garlic, Italian seasoning, salt, and pepper. Pulse to finely chop the mixture, but don't puree it. Transfer the mixture to a medium bowl.

4. Stir the eggs into the lentil mixture. Form the mixture into walnut-size balls and arrange them on the prepared baking sheet about 1 inch apart.

5. Brush the "meatballs" with the oil.

6. Bake for about 35 minutes, until golden brown. Serve immediately or store in the refrigerator for up to 3 days.

Optional Finishing Touch: Sprinkle with chopped fresh basil or freshly grated Parmesan cheese.

Pairing Tip: Serve these vegetarian meatballs on top of spaghetti with Marinara Sauce (page 165).

Per serving: Calories: 370; Total Fat: 20g; Saturated Fat: 4g; Cholesterol: 188mg; Sodium: 656mg; Total Carbohydrates: 29g; Sugars: 2g; Protein: 19g

BAKED PASTA WITH WHITE BEANS

SERVES 2 / PREP TIME: 10 MINUTES / COOK TIME: 45 MINUTES

Baked pasta is easy to change by adding fresh herbs like basil or oregano or vegetables like diced zucchini or mushrooms or chopped spinach.

OLIVE OIL OR NONSTICK
COOKING SPRAY, FOR
PREPARING THE PAN

4 OUNCES FUSILLI OR
ROTINI PASTA

2 CUPS MARINARA
SAUCE (PAGE 165) OR
STORE-BOUGHT

1 CUP CANNED WHITE
BEANS, DRAINED
AND RINSED

½ CUP WHOLE-MILK
RICOTTA CHEESE

½ CUP SHREDDED
MOZZARELLA CHEESE

1. Preheat the oven to 350°F. Brush or spray an 8-inch square baking dish with oil.

2. Bring a medium pot of water to a boil and cook the pasta according to the package directions until al dente. Drain.

3. In the prepared baking dish, stir together the sauce, pasta, and beans. Spread the mixture into an even layer in the baking dish.

4. Dollop the ricotta cheese on top.

5. Cover the dish with aluminum foil and bake for about 30 minutes, until the sauce is bubbling.

6. Remove the foil from the baking dish, sprinkle the mozzarella cheese over the top, and bake for 10 minutes more, until the cheese is melted and beginning to brown. Serve hot.

Flavor Tip: To add more flavor to this dish, instead of using mozzarella, look for an Italian cheese blend. Such blends often include a combination of provolone, Asiago, mozzarella, and other cheeses.

Per serving: Calories: 540; Total Fat: 13g; Saturated Fat: 7g; Cholesterol: 31mg; Sodium: 1,240mg; Total Carbohydrates: 82g; Sugars: 12g; Protein: 29g

PASTA WITH GOAT CHEESE AND ASPARAGUS

30 MINUTES OR LESS **FEELING FANCY**

SERVES 2 / PREP TIME: 5 MINUTES / COOK TIME: 20 MINUTES

This gorgeous pasta dish combines tangy, creamy goat cheese with bright fresh asparagus. Cooking the pasta on the stovetop while the asparagus is roasting in the oven means that this dish can easily be on the table in under 30 minutes.

1 POUND ASPARAGUS, TRIMMED, CUT ON AN ANGLE INTO ⅛-INCH-THICK SLICES

1 TABLESPOON OLIVE OIL

1 TEASPOON KOSHER SALT, PLUS MORE IF NEEDED

½ TEASPOON FRESHLY GROUND BLACK PEPPER, PLUS MORE IF NEEDED

8 OUNCES PASTA

2 OUNCES GOAT CHEESE

¼ CUP HEAVY (WHIPPING) CREAM

GRATED ZEST AND JUICE OF 1 SMALL LEMON

1. Preheat the oven to 450°F. Line a baking sheet with parchment paper or aluminum foil.

2. Arrange the asparagus on the prepared baking sheet and toss with the oil. Season with the salt and pepper. Roast the asparagus until tender, about 10 minutes.

3. Meanwhile, bring a medium pot of salted water to a boil and cook the pasta according to the package directions until al dente. Drain, reserving 1 cup of the cooking water.

4. Return the pasta cooking pot to the stovetop over medium heat. Add the cheese and cream and cook, stirring, until the cheese melts and the sauce is incorporated. Add the lemon zest and juice, asparagus, and cooked pasta and stir until the pasta is coated. If necessary, add a bit of the pasta cooking water to thin the sauce. Taste and adjust the seasoning if necessary. Serve hot.

Optional Finishing Touch: Garnish with freshly grated Parmesan cheese, red pepper flakes, or both.

Per serving: Calories: 684; Total Fat: 26g; Saturated Fat: 12g; Cholesterol: 54mg; Sodium: 415mg; Total Carbohydrates: 91g; Sugars: 5g; Protein: 25g

EGGPLANT PARMESAN
WITH PESTO

30 MINUTES OR LESS

SERVES 2 / PREP TIME: 5 MINUTES / COOK TIME: 20 MINUTES

Eggplant Parmesan typically involves the laborious process of dredging and pan-frying slices of eggplant. This recipe skips the panfrying. Instead, the eggplant is simply halved and roasted, then topped with pesto and cheesy bread crumbs.

1 SMALL EGGPLANT

2 TABLESPOONS OLIVE OIL

½ TEASPOON KOSHER SALT

¼ CUP HERB PESTO
   (PAGE 163) OR
   STORE-BOUGHT

¼ CUP PANKO
   BREAD CRUMBS

¼ CUP SHREDDED
   MOZZARELLA CHEESE

2 TABLESPOONS GRATED
   PARMESAN CHEESE

1. Preheat the oven to 400°F. Line a rimmed baking sheet with aluminum foil or parchment paper.

2. Cut the eggplant in half lengthwise, then score the cut side of each half with a crosshatch pattern about ½ inch deep. Place the eggplant halves on the prepared baking sheet, cut-side up. Drizzle the oil over the eggplant and season with the salt.

3. Bake for about 30 minutes, until the eggplant is tender. Remove the pan from the oven and raise the oven temperature to 475°F.

4. Spread the pesto over the cut sides of the eggplant.

5. In a small bowl, toss together the bread crumbs, mozzarella, and Parmesan. Sprinkle the mixture over the eggplant halves.

6. Bake for about 5 minutes, until the cheese is melted, bubbling, and browned. Serve hot.

Variation: If you prefer more of the traditional eggplant Parmesan flavor, substitute 1 cup Marinara Sauce (page 165) for the pesto.

Per serving: Calories: 410; Total Fat: 32g; Saturated Fat: 7g; Cholesterol: 20mg; Sodium: 821mg; Total Carbohydrates: 24g; Sugars: 9g; Protein: 12g

Spicy Crab Cakes, page 86

Chapter Six

SEAFOOD

HONEY GARLIC SHRIMP

30 MINUTES OR LESS

SERVES 2 / PREP TIME: 5 MINUTES, PLUS 15 MINUTES
TO MARINATE / COOK TIME: 10 MINUTES

This sweet and savory shrimp takes just about 30 minutes to get on the table. Serve it over steamed rice or quinoa with a side of steamed or sautéed veggies.

¼ CUP HONEY

2 TABLESPOONS SOY SAUCE

JUICE OF ½ LEMON

1 GARLIC CLOVE, MINCED

8 OUNCES PEELED AND
  DEVEINED SHRIMP

2 TABLESPOONS OLIVE OIL

KOSHER SALT

FRESHLY GROUND
  BLACK PEPPER

1. In a small bowl, whisk together the honey, soy sauce, lemon juice, and garlic.

2. In a medium bowl, toss together the shrimp and half the sauce (reserve the remaining sauce for later). Cover and refrigerate for 15 minutes.

3. In a medium skillet, heat the oil over medium-high heat. Add the shrimp, discarding the marinade. Add a pinch each of salt and pepper and cook, turning occasionally, for about 4 minutes, until the shrimp are cooked through.

4. Pour the reserved sauce over the shrimp and cook, stirring, until the sauce thickens, about 3 minutes more. Serve hot.

Optional Finishing Touch: Garnish with sliced scallions.

Cooking Tip: Don't waste time peeling and deveining shrimp yourself. Buy already peeled and deveined shrimp from the market.

Per serving: Calories: 335; Total Fat: 14g; Saturated Fat: 2g; Cholesterol: 120mg; Sodium: 927mg; Total Carbohydrates: 37g; Sugars: 36g; Protein: 19g

SHRIMP WITH FETA, TOMATOES, AND MINT

FEELING FANCY　**ONE POT**

**SERVES 2 / PREP TIME: 5 MINUTES, PLUS 15 MINUTES
TO MARINATE / COOK TIME: 20 MINUTES**

This Greek-inspired shrimp dish will seriously wow you with its robust flavor. The combination of tomatoes, shrimp, feta cheese, and fresh mint is simply divine.

1 TABLESPOON OLIVE OIL

1 GARLIC CLOVE, MINCED

1 (14.5-OUNCE) CAN DICED
   TOMATOES

12 OUNCES PEELED AND
   DEVEINED SHRIMP

¼ TEASPOON KOSHER SALT

¼ TEASPOON FRESHLY
   GROUND BLACK PEPPER

⅓ CUP CRUMBLED
   FETA CHEESE

2 TABLESPOONS CHOPPED
   FRESH MINT

1. Preheat the oven to 425°F.

2. In an oven-safe skillet, heat the oil over medium-high heat. Add the garlic and cook, stirring, for 1 minute. Add the tomatoes and their juices and bring to a boil. Reduce the heat to medium-low and simmer for about 5 minutes, until the sauce thickens.

3. Remove the pan from the heat and add the shrimp, stirring to coat. Season with the salt and pepper. Sprinkle the cheese over the top.

4. Bake for 12 to 14 minutes, until the cheese is melted and the shrimp are fully cooked. Serve hot, garnished with the mint.

Pairing Tip: You can serve this dish with crusty bread, but it would also be tasty alone or over pasta or rice.

*Per serving: Calories: 273; Total Fat: 13g; Saturated Fat: 5g; Cholesterol: 202mg; Sodium: 917mg;
Total Carbohydrates: 10g; Sugars: 7g; Protein: 33g*

SPICY CRAB CAKES

30 MINUTES OR LESS   **FEELING FANCY**

SERVES 2 / PREP TIME: 5 MINUTES / COOK TIME: 10 MINUTES

Crab cakes are definitely a special meal dish in my book. But that doesn't mean they have to be time-consuming to make or require a lot of ingredients. These crab cakes can be on the table in 15 minutes. Add a salad of mixed greens with vinaigrette dressing and you'll feel like you're in a fancy bistro.

1 LARGE EGG,
   LIGHTLY BEATEN

2 TABLESPOONS
   MAYONNAISE

1½ TEASPOONS CAJUN
   SPICE MIX (I LIKE TONY
   CHACHERE'S)

8 OUNCES LUMP CRABMEAT

½ CUP PANKO
   BREAD CRUMBS

1 TABLESPOON OLIVE OIL

1. In a medium bowl, whisk together the egg, mayonnaise, and spice mix.

2. Add the crab and bread crumbs and stir to mix well.

3. Form the mixture into ½-inch-thick patties, about 3 inches in diameter.

4. In a large skillet, heat the oil over medium heat until sizzling. Add the crab cakes and cook for about 4 minutes, until golden brown on the bottom. Flip the crab cakes over and cook for another 4 minutes or so, until the second side is golden brown. Serve hot.

Pairing Tip: For a dipping sauce, make a quick garlic aioli by stirring together mayonnaise and minced garlic.

Per serving: Calories: 371; Total Fat: 22g; Saturated Fat: 4g; Cholesterol: 211mg; Sodium: 588mg; Total Carbohydrates: 15g; Sugars: 1g; Protein: 28g

LINGUINE WITH CLAM SAUCE

30 MINUTES OR LESS   FEELING FANCY

SERVES 2 / PREP TIME: 5 MINUTES / COOK TIME: 10 MINUTES

This dish feels special but is still quick and easy to make. If you can, buy small, fresh clams (I like Manila clams), and keep them in the refrigerator in an open plastic bag or completely submerged in a bowl of cold water until you are ready to cook them.

8 OUNCES LINGUINE

3 TABLESPOONS OLIVE OIL

2 GARLIC CLOVES, MINCED

1 POUND SMALL CLAMS
(ABOUT 2 DOZEN),
SCRUBBED

1 CUP DRY WHITE WINE,
SUCH AS PINOT GRIGIO,
CHARDONNAY, OR
SAUVIGNON BLANC

3 TABLESPOONS
FINELY CHOPPED
FRESH FLAT-LEAF
PARSLEY, DIVIDED

½ TEASPOON KOSHER SALT,
PLUS MORE IF NEEDED

1. Bring a large pot of water to a boil and cook the pasta according to the package directions until al dente. Drain, reserving ½ cup of the cooking water. Set aside.

2. Meanwhile, in a large skillet, heat the oil over medium-high heat. Add the garlic and cook, stirring, for about 30 seconds. Add the clams, wine, 2 tablespoons of the parsley, and the salt. Bring the mixture to a simmer, then reduce the heat to low, cover, and cook for about 7 minutes, until the clams are open (discard any that don't open).

3. Add the pasta to the skillet and raise the heat to medium. Cook, tossing occasionally, until most of the sauce has been absorbed by the pasta, about 2 minutes. If the pan is too dry, add a little of the reserved pasta cooking water.

⟶

4. Remove the pan from the heat and stir in the remaining 1 tablespoon parsley. Taste and add more salt, if needed. Serve immediately.

Flavor Tip: Boost the flavor further by stirring in 2 tablespoons butter and the zest and juice of ½ lemon before serving.

Variation: If you can't find fresh clams, you can substitute canned. The dish won't present as fancy without the shells, but the taste will still be great. Add the clams and their juices when you add the wine, and reduce the cooking time in the first step to 4 to 5 minutes.

Per serving: Calories: 730; Total Fat: 23g; Saturated Fat: 3g; Cholesterol: 12mg; Sodium: 610mg; Total Carbohydrates: 87g; Sugars: 5g; Protein: 19g

MISO-GLAZED SALMON

FEELING FANCY

**SERVES 2 / PREP TIME: 5 MINUTES, PLUS 30 MINUTES
TO MARINATE / COOK TIME: 10 MINUTES**

This dish is a magical combination of super delicious and really easy to make. It makes frequent appearances at my house, and no one in my family ever complains—that's how I know when something is especially tasty.

1½ TABLESPOONS WHITE
  MISO PASTE

1 TABLESPOON SAKE

1 TABLESPOON SUGAR

1 TABLESPOON SOY SAUCE

2 (5- TO 6-OUNCE)
  SALMON FILLETS

1. In a medium bowl, mix together the miso, sake, sugar, and soy sauce until smooth.

2. Add the salmon fillets and turn to coat. Cover and refrigerate for 30 minutes.

3. Preheat the oven to 450°F.

4. Transfer the salmon fillets to a baking dish and pour any extra marinade over the top.

5. Bake for about 10 minutes, until the fish flakes easily with a fork and the sauce has thickened and browned in places.

Optional Finishing Touch: Garnish with thinly sliced scallions, toasted sesame seeds, or both.

Pairing Tip: Serve with steamed rice and veggies for a healthy and satisfying meal.

Per serving: Calories: 370; Total Fat: 19g; Saturated Fat: 4g; Cholesterol: 100mg; Sodium: 990mg; Total Carbohydrates: 10g; Sugars: 7g; Protein: 36g

ROASTED CHILI-LIME SEA BASS

30 MINUTES OR LESS

SERVES 2 / PREP TIME: 5 MINUTES / COOK TIME: 12 MINUTES

This Mexican-influenced roasted fish is delightful on its own or as the filling for healthy fish tacos. Serve with lime wedges to squeeze over the fish at the table.

2 TABLESPOONS UNSALTED
   BUTTER, MELTED
1 TEASPOON CHILI
   POWDER (PAGE 160) OR
   STORE-BOUGHT
1 SMALL GARLIC
   CLOVE, MINCED
½ TEASPOON KOSHER SALT
JUICE OF 1 LIME
2 (5- TO 6-OUNCE) SEA
   BASS FILLETS

1. Preheat the oven to 425°F.

2. In a small bowl, whisk together the butter, chili powder, garlic, and salt. Stir in the lime juice.

3. Arrange the fish in a baking dish and pour the sauce over the top.

4. Roast the fish for 10 to 12 minutes, until it is cooked through and flakes easily with a fork. Serve immediately.

Pairing Tip: Pair with warm corn tortillas, Fresh Salsa Picante (page 162) or store-bought salsa fresca, and shredded lettuce or cabbage, as preferred.

Per serving: Calories: 278; Total Fat: 16g; Saturated Fat: 7g; Cholesterol: 101mg; Sodium: 714mg; Total Carbohydrates: 3g; Sugars: 1g; Protein: 33g

COD COOKED IN PARCHMENT WITH TOMATOES, CHILES, AND CILANTRO

SERVES 2 / PREP TIME: 10 MINUTES / COOK TIME: 25 MINUTES

Cooking fish in parchment paper is genius. It ensures that your fish is tender, juicy, and deeply infused with the flavors of the sauce or other ingredients you've cooked it with. Bonus: Cooking in parchment makes for a cool presentation and super-easy cleanup.

1 (15-OUNCE) CAN FIRE-ROASTED DICED TOMATOES WITH GREEN CHILES, DRAINED

1 JALAPEÑO PEPPER, DICED (SEEDED FOR A MILDER DISH)

1 SMALL GARLIC CLOVE, MINCED

2 (6-OUNCE) COD FILLETS

KOSHER SALT

FRESHLY GROUND BLACK PEPPER

3 TEASPOONS OLIVE OIL

2 TABLESPOONS CHOPPED FRESH CILANTRO

1. Preheat the oven to 425°F. Prepare 2 (16-inch) squares of parchment paper.

2. In a large bowl, mix together the tomatoes, jalapeño, and garlic.

3. Place a fish fillet on each parchment sheet, positioning it on half of the sheet and leaving room to fold the other half over the fish. Season generously with salt and pepper. Spoon the tomato mixture over the fish, dividing it equally. Drizzle 1½ teaspoons of the oil over each fillet.

4. Fold the parchment over the fish and crimp the edges all the way around to seal the packet, leaving room for steam to accumulate inside. Place the sealed packets on a baking sheet.

⟶

5. Bake for 25 minutes. Remove the pan from the oven and let the packets rest for 5 minutes before opening them.

6. To serve, open the packets and sprinkle the cilantro over the fish. Serve immediately.

Optional Finishing Touch: Serve with lemon wedges for squeezing over the fish.

Pairing Tip: Serve with Rice Pilaf with Almonds and Raisins (page 156).

Per serving: Calories: 218; Total Fat: 9g; Saturated Fat: 1g; Cholesterol: 83mg; Sodium: 371mg; Total Carbohydrates: 5g; Sugars: 3g; Protein: 31g

ITALIAN-STYLE OVEN-BAKED FISH

30 MINUTES OR LESS **FEELING FANCY** **ONE PAN**

SERVES 2 / PREP TIME: 5 MINUTES / COOK TIME: 15 MINUTES

Kalamata olives and Italian herb–flavored tomatoes give this dish a Mediterranean flair. Try it over cooked rice, orzo pasta, or couscous.

1 TABLESPOON OLIVE OIL

1 GARLIC CLOVE, MINCED

1 (15-OUNCE) CAN DICED TOMATOES WITH ITALIAN HERBS, DRAINED

2 TABLESPOONS CHOPPED KALAMATA OLIVES

½ TEASPOON RED PEPPER FLAKES

2 (6-OUNCE) WHITE FISH FILLETS (COD, SEA BASS, TILAPIA, OR ANY MILD WHITE FISH WILL WORK)

KOSHER SALT

FRESHLY GROUND BLACK PEPPER

1. Preheat the oven to 375°F.

2. In a large ovenproof skillet, heat the oil over medium-high heat. Add the garlic and cook, stirring, for about 30 seconds.

3. Add the tomatoes, olives, and red pepper flakes and cook, stirring occasionally, until most of the liquid has evaporated, about 5 minutes.

4. Season the fish with salt and pepper and add the fillets to the skillet, nestling them into the tomatoes.

5. Transfer the skillet to the oven and bake for about 10 minutes, until the fish is cooked through and flakes easily with a fork. Serve immediately.

Variation: Give this dish a Spanish twist by sautéing diced cured Spanish chorizo in the skillet before adding the garlic.

Per serving: Calories: 231; Total Fat: 10g; Saturated Fat: 1g; Cholesterol: 83mg; Sodium: 406mg; Total Carbohydrates: 6g; Sugars: 2g; Protein: 31g

WEEKNIGHT FISH TACOS

30 MINUTES OR LESS

SERVES 2 / PREP TIME: 5 MINUTES / COOK TIME: 15 MINUTES

You can't go too wrong with tacos, and these easy fish tacos are always well received. This preparation includes crunchy cabbage and a creamy sauce made by mixing together sour cream and spicy salsa. It's one of those simple cheats that really elevates a dish.

½ CUP SOUR CREAM

½ CUP FRESH SALSA
PICANTE (PAGE 162)
OR STORE-BOUGHT
SPICY SALSA

2 (6-OUNCE) WHITE-
FLESHED FISH FILLETS
(COD, TILAPIA, SEA BASS,
OR SIMILAR FISH)

1 TABLESPOON OLIVE OIL

KOSHER SALT

FRESHLY GROUND
BLACK PEPPER

8 CORN TORTILLAS

1 CUP SHREDDED
RED CABBAGE

1. Preheat the broiler to high.

2. In a small bowl, stir together the sour cream and salsa.

3. Place the fish fillets on a baking sheet and drizzle the oil over them. Season generously with salt and pepper.

4. Broil until the fish is cooked through, flakes easily with a fork, and is beginning to brown on top.

5. Heat the tortillas on a griddle or skillet or directly over the flame of a gas stovetop.

6. Divide the fish evenly among the tortillas. Drizzle the sour cream mixture over the fish, then top each taco with a handful of cabbage.

Optional Finishing Touch: Tacos can be dressed up with any number of toppings. Sprinkle a bit of chopped fresh cilantro over the fish and add diced avocado or a squeeze of lime juice.

Flavor Tip: You can also bake the fish fillets with a simple bread crumb crust for a crunchy taco filling.

Per serving: Calories: 554; Total Fat: 23g; Saturated Fat: 9g; Cholesterol: 108mg; Sodium: 653mg; Total Carbohydrates: 51g; Sugars: 4g; Protein: 39g

PAN-SEARED FISH WITH TOMATILLO SAUCE

30 MINUTES OR LESS

SERVES 2 / PREP TIME: 5 MINUTES / COOK TIME: 15 MINUTES

This Mexican-inspired fish dish uses tomatillos, lime juice, and pickled jalapeños. It makes a great filling for tacos and is also delicious served on its own or with rice.

4 OUNCES TOMATILLOS, HUSKS REMOVED, RINSED, AND HALVED OR QUARTERED

½ CUP CHOPPED FRESH CILANTRO, PLUS MORE FOR GARNISH

2 TABLESPOONS CHOPPED PICKLED JALAPEÑOS

KOSHER SALT

2 (6-OUNCE) WHITE-FLESHED FISH FILLETS (COD, TILAPIA, SEA BASS, OR SIMILAR FISH)

½ TEASPOON GROUND CUMIN

2 TABLESPOONS OLIVE OIL

1. In a blender, combine the tomatillos, cilantro, and jalapeños and puree. Season with salt to taste.

2. Season the fish generously with salt and sprinkle with the cumin.

3. In a large heavy skillet (ideally cast iron), heat the oil over medium-high heat. Cook the fish until browned on the bottom, 3 to 4 minutes. Flip the fish over and cook until cooked through and browned on the second side, about 4 minutes more.

4. Divide the sauce between two wide, shallow serving bowls or plates. Arrange the fish fillets on top of the sauce and garnish with cilantro. Serve hot.

Pairing Tip: Serve this saucy fish with warm corn tortillas and crumbled fresh Mexican cheese or feta cheese, if you decide to go the taco route.

Per serving: Calories: 286; Total Fat: 17g; Saturated Fat: 2g; Cholesterol: 83mg; Sodium: 646mg; Total Carbohydrates: 5g; Sugars: 0g; Protein: 31g

Shredded Chicken Tacos with Corn Salsa, page 100

Chapter Seven

POULTRY

CRISPY CHICKEN WITH WHITE BEANS AND PESTO

30 MINUTES OR LESS **ONE PAN**

SERVES 2 / PREP TIME: 5 MINUTES / COOK TIME: 20 MINUTES

This one-pan meal is super easy to make. The beans and kale are cooked together in the chicken drippings before prepared pesto is added.

2 TABLESPOONS OLIVE OIL, DIVIDED

2 SKIN-ON, BONELESS CHICKEN THIGHS (ABOUT 8 OUNCES)

½ TEASPOON KOSHER SALT, PLUS MORE AS NEEDED

¼ TEASPOON FRESHLY GROUND BLACK PEPPER, PLUS MORE AS NEEDED

1 MEDIUM SHALLOT, THINLY SLICED

4 CUPS CHOPPED KALE

1 (15-OUNCE) CAN CANNELLINI BEANS, DRAINED AND RINSED

⅓ CUP HERB PESTO (PAGE 163) OR STORE-BOUGHT

1. In a large skillet, heat 1 tablespoon of the oil over high heat.

2. Season the chicken with the salt and pepper and add it to the pan, skin-side down. Cook for about 2 minutes, then reduce the heat to medium-high. Cook for about 5 minutes more, until the skin is crisp and golden brown. Turn the chicken over and cook for 3 to 4 minutes more, until cooked through. Remove the chicken from the skillet.

3. Raise the heat back to high and add the remaining 1 tablespoon oil to the skillet. Add the shallot and cook, stirring occasionally, for about 3 minutes, until softened. Add the kale and cook for about 2 minutes more, until wilted. Add the beans and cook, stirring, until the beans are heated through and the kale is tender, about 3 minutes more. Stir in the pesto and season with salt and pepper.

4. Place the chicken on top of the beans and serve immediately.

Optional Finishing Touch: Garnish with freshly grated Parmesan cheese and chopped fresh parsley.

Per serving: Calories: 789; Total Fat: 52g; Saturated Fat: 11g; Cholesterol: 111mg; Sodium: 877mg; Total Carbohydrates: 48g; Sugars: 3g; Protein: 37g

GREEK LEMON CHICKEN WITH OLIVES

SERVES 2 / PREP TIME: 5 MINUTES / COOK TIME: 1 HOUR

In this recipe, the chicken skin gets nicely browned and crisp. Fresh lemon juice, olives, and oregano give the chicken a light but intense flavor. Drizzle the pan juices over the chicken before serving.

2 BONE-IN, SKIN-ON
   CHICKEN LEG QUARTERS
   (THIGH AND DRUMSTICK)

¼ CUP PITTED
   GREEK OLIVES

2 TABLESPOONS OLIVE OIL

1 TABLESPOON FRESHLY
   SQUEEZED LEMON JUICE

1 GARLIC CLOVE, MINCED

½ TEASPOON KOSHER SALT

½ TEASPOON FRESHLY
   GROUND BLACK PEPPER

½ TEASPOON
   DRIED OREGANO

1. Preheat the oven to 375°F.

2. In an 8-inch square baking dish, arrange the chicken and scatter the olives over the top.

3. In a small bowl, combine the oil, lemon juice, garlic, salt, pepper, and oregano and stir to mix. Pour the mixture over the chicken and olives in the baking dish.

4. Bake for about 1 hour, until the chicken skin is browned and crisp and the chicken is cooked through. Serve hot.

Cooking Tip: Make this an even heartier meal by placing a base layer of cubed potatoes (1 or 2 medium potatoes) in the bottom of the baking dish. Arrange the chicken on top and proceed with the recipe as written. Add 10 to 15 minutes to the cooking time.

Storage Tip: This dish freezes well. After cooking, let it cool to room temperature, then transfer it to a freezer-safe resealable plastic bag or other freezer-safe storage container and store in the freezer for up to 3 months. To serve, thaw in the refrigerator overnight and reheat in the microwave.

Per serving: Calories: 367; Total Fat: 33g; Saturated Fat: 9g; Cholesterol: 98mg; Sodium: 687mg; Total Carbohydrates: 2g; Sugars: 0g; Protein: 17g

SHREDDED CHICKEN TACOS WITH CORN SALSA

30 MINUTES OR LESS **ONE PAN**

SERVES 2 / PREP TIME: 5 MINUTES / COOK TIME: 5 MINUTES

If you've got cooked chicken in the refrigerator, this delicious dinner can be on the table in under 10 minutes. You can always pick up a rotisserie chicken on the way home, or prepare a couple of chicken breasts on an outdoor grill or in a grill pan on the stove.

8 OUNCES SHREDDED COOKED CHICKEN

1 CUP FRESH OR FROZEN CORN KERNELS (THAWED, IF FROZEN)

½ CUP SALSA (MILD, MEDIUM, OR HOT)

4 CORN TORTILLAS

½ CUP SHREDDED MEXICAN-STYLE CHEESE BLEND

1. In a large saucepan, combine the chicken, corn, and salsa and bring to a simmer over medium heat. Cook, stirring, for 1 to 2 minutes, until heated through.

2. Heat the tortillas on a griddle or skillet or directly over the flame on a gas stovetop.

3. Divide the chicken mixture evenly between the tortillas and top with the cheese. Serve immediately.

Optional Finishing Touch: Top with sour cream, guacamole or diced avocado, diced red onions, chopped fresh cilantro, or hot sauce.

Pairing Tip: These tacos work well with refried beans, Mexican-style rice, or both on the side.

Per serving: Calories: 368; Total Fat: 15g; Saturated Fat: 7g; Cholesterol: 112mg; Sodium: 695mg; Total Carbohydrates: 41g; Sugars: 5g; Protein: 45g

ROSEMARY CHICKEN
WITH POTATOES

SERVES 2 / PREP TIME: 5 MINUTES / COOK TIME: 1 HOUR

Fresh, aromatic rosemary and garlic flavor these chicken leg quarters, which are baked in the oven along with potatoes. Everything crisps to a perfect golden brown. Serve with a vegetable on the side, if you like.

2 RUSSET POTATOES, CUBED

1½ TABLESPOONS OLIVE OIL

2 TEASPOONS CHOPPED
  FRESH ROSEMARY

1 GARLIC CLOVE, MINCED

½ TEASPOON KOSHER SALT

2 BONE-IN, SKIN-ON
  CHICKEN LEG QUARTERS
  (THIGH AND DRUMSTICK)

1. Preheat the oven to 375°F.

2. Arrange the potatoes in the bottom of an 8-inch square baking dish.

3. In a small bowl, mix together the oil, rosemary, garlic, and salt. Spread the mixture all over the chicken thighs, then arrange the chicken on top of the potatoes.

4. Bake for 1 hour to 1 hour 15 minutes, until the chicken skin is browned and crisp and the chicken is cooked through. Serve hot.

Optional Finishing Touch: Add a squeeze of lemon juice and a handful of toasted pine nuts for extra flavor.

Pairing Tip: Serve with sautéed or steamed green beans, with a light drizzle of melted butter.

Per serving: Calories: 475; Total Fat: 30g; Saturated Fat: 8g; Cholesterol: 98mg; Sodium: 664mg; Total Carbohydrates: 34g; Sugars: 3g; Protein: 21g

HONEY MUSTARD CHICKEN THIGHS

SERVES 2 / PREP TIME: 5 MINUTES / COOK TIME: 40 MINUTES

The sweet and savory combination of honey and mustard is always a hit. This dish is easy to put together—just whisk the sauce ingredients in a bowl, toss in the thighs, then bake them. They are delicious served over roasted potatoes, couscous, or rice.

NONSTICK COOKING SPRAY

2½ TABLESPOONS HONEY

2 TABLESPOONS WHOLE-GRAIN MUSTARD

1 TABLESPOON DIJON MUSTARD

1 TABLESPOON OLIVE OIL

8 TO 12 OUNCES BONELESS, SKINLESS CHICKEN BREAST OR THIGH MEAT, CUT INTO 2-INCH PIECES

½ TEASPOON KOSHER SALT

½ TEASPOON FRESHLY GROUND BLACK PEPPER

1. Preheat the oven to 375°F. Spray an 8-inch square baking dish with cooking spray.

2. In a medium bowl, whisk together the honey, whole-grain and Dijon mustards, and oil. Add the chicken, salt, and pepper and toss to coat.

3. Transfer the chicken and sauce to the prepared baking dish and spread it out in a single layer.

4. Cover the baking dish with aluminum foil and bake for 30 minutes. Remove the foil and bake for 10 minutes more. Serve hot.

Optional Finishing Touch: You can mix together ½ cup bread crumbs and 1 tablespoon melted butter, and spread it over the chicken after removing the foil. Bake for the remaining 10 minutes, uncovered, until the bread crumbs are golden brown and crisp.

Storage Tip: This dish freezes well. After cooking, let it cool to room temperature, then transfer it to a freezer-safe resealable plastic bag or other freezer-safe storage container and store in the freezer for up to 3 months. To serve, thaw in the refrigerator overnight and reheat in the microwave.

Per serving: Calories: 370; Total Fat: 15g; Saturated Fat: 3g; Cholesterol: 109mg; Sodium: 958mg; Total Carbohydrates: 22g; Sugars: 21g; Protein: 38g

SPICED CHICKEN WITH TOMATOES

FREEZER-FRIENDLY   **ONE POT**

SERVES 2 / PREP TIME: 5 MINUTES / COOK TIME: 1 HOUR 45 MINUTES

A hint of cinnamon in this dish is delightfully unexpected, and the flavor strikes a perfect balance between the sweetness of the tomatoes and the tang of the lemon juice. Serve this chicken with rice, pasta, or roasted potatoes.

2 BONE-IN, SKIN-ON
   CHICKEN LEG QUARTERS
   (THIGH AND DRUMSTICK)
½ TEASPOON KOSHER SALT
½ TEASPOON FRESHLY
   GROUND BLACK PEPPER
2 TABLESPOONS OLIVE OIL
1 SHALLOT, THINLY SLICED
1 (14.5-OUNCE) CAN DICED
   TOMATOES
¼ TEASPOON GROUND
   CINNAMON
1 TABLESPOON FRESHLY
   SQUEEZED LEMON JUICE

1. Season the chicken with the salt and pepper.

2. In a Dutch oven, heat the oil over medium-high heat. Add the chicken, skin-side down, and cook for about 6 minutes, until the skin is golden brown and crisp. Turn the chicken over and cook for 3 to 4 minutes more, until the second side is browned. Remove the chicken from the pot, transferring it to a plate.

3. Add the shallot to the pot and cook, stirring, for about 6 minutes, until softened and beginning to brown.

4. Stir in the tomatoes and their juices and the cinnamon and cook for about 6 minutes more, until the tomatoes begin to break down.

5. Return the chicken to the pot, along with any juices that have accumulated on the plate. Cover, reduce the heat to low, and cook for 45 to 50 minutes, until the chicken is cooked through.

6. Remove the lid from the pot and simmer until the chicken is very tender and easily pulls away from the bone, another 45 minutes or so.

7. Stir in the lemon juice just before serving. Serve hot.

Optional Finishing Touch: Garnish with a sprinkling of chopped fresh cilantro for added flavor and color.

Storage Tip: This dish freezes well. After cooking, let it cool to room temperature, then transfer it to a freezer-safe storage container and store in the freezer for up to 3 months. To serve, thaw in the refrigerator overnight and reheat in the microwave.

Per serving: Calories: 401; Total Fat: 33g; Saturated Fat: 9g; Cholesterol: 98mg; Sodium: 664mg; Total Carbohydrates: 10g; Sugars: 6g; Protein: 19g

APPLE CIDER-BRAISED CHICKEN

FREEZER-FRIENDLY **ONE POT**

SERVES 2 / PREP TIME: 5 MINUTES / COOK TIME: 1 HOUR 15 MINUTES

This apple-scented chicken dish is perfect for chilly fall evenings. It takes a while to cook, but most of that time is hands-off. Serve this chicken with garlic mashed or roasted potatoes and a green vegetable.

2 BONE-IN, SKIN-ON
 CHICKEN LEG QUARTERS
 (THIGH AND DRUMSTICK)
½ TEASPOON KOSHER SALT
½ TEASPOON FRESHLY
 GROUND BLACK PEPPER
1 TABLESPOON OLIVE OIL
1 SHALLOT, THINLY SLICED
2 TABLESPOONS APPLE
 CIDER VINEGAR
½ CUP CHICKEN BROTH
½ CUP APPLE CIDER

1. Season the chicken pieces with the salt and pepper.

2. In a Dutch oven, heat the oil over medium-high heat. Add the chicken, skin-side down, and cook for about 6 minutes, until the skin is golden brown and crisp. Turn the chicken over and cook for 3 to 4 minutes more, until the second side is browned. Remove the chicken from the pot, transferring it to a plate.

3. Add the shallot to the pot and cook, stirring frequently, for about 5 minutes, until softened.

4. Add the vinegar and cook, stirring and scraping up any browned bits that have stuck to the bottom of the pan, for about 1 minute. Add the broth and cider and bring to a boil.

5. Reduce the heat to low and return the chicken and any accumulated juices to the pot. Cover the pot and cook at a low simmer for about 30 minutes.

6. Turn the chicken pieces over and cook, uncovered, for about 30 minutes more, until the chicken is cooked through.

Flavor Tip: Add a cored, peeled, and diced apple to the pot along with the shallot for extra flavor and texture.

Storage Tip: This dish freezes well. After cooking, let it cool to room temperature, then transfer it to a freezer-safe storage container and store in the freezer for up to 3 months. To serve, thaw in the refrigerator overnight and reheat in the microwave.

Per serving: Calories: 343; Total Fat: 26g; Saturated Fat: 8g; Cholesterol: 98mg; Sodium: 746mg; Total Carbohydrates: 9g; Sugars: 7g; Protein: 18g

CHICKEN TIKKA MASALA

**SERVES 2 / PREP TIME: 5 MINUTES, PLUS 30 MINUTES
TO MARINATE / COOK TIME: 15 MINUTES**

Marinating chicken in yogurt makes it incredibly tender and helps it absorb all the yummy flavors in the curry paste. Keeping a jar of Indian curry paste in the refrigerator makes it easy to whip up delicious Indian-style meals like this one in a flash. Serve over steamed basmati rice.

3 TABLESPOONS MASALA
   CURRY PASTE, DIVIDED

¼ CUP FULL-FAT
   PLAIN YOGURT

1 POUND BONELESS,
   SKINLESS CHICKEN
   BREAST OR THIGH, CUT
   INTO BITE-SIZE PIECES

1 TABLESPOON OLIVE OIL

1 CUP TOMATO SAUCE

½ TEASPOON KOSHER SALT

½ CUP HEAVY (WHIPPING)
   CREAM OR FULL-FAT
   COCONUT MILK

1. In a medium bowl, stir together 1½ tablespoons of the curry paste and the yogurt. Add the chicken and toss to coat. Refrigerate for at least 30 minutes.

2. In a large skillet, heat the oil over medium-high heat. Remove the chicken from the marinade, discarding the marinade, and add the meat to the skillet. Cook, stirring occasionally, until the chicken is browned all over, about 5 minutes.

3. Stir the remaining 1½ tablespoons curry paste, the tomato sauce, and the salt into the skillet and reduce the heat to medium-low. Cook, stirring occasionally, for about 10 minutes, until the chicken is cooked through and the sauce is thick.

4. Stir in the cream and serve immediately.

Optional Finishing Touch: Garnish with chopped fresh cilantro.

Storage Tip: This dish freezes well. Cook according to the instructions through step 3. Let it cool to room temperature, then transfer it to a freezer-safe storage container and store in the freezer for up to 3 months. To serve, thaw in the refrigerator overnight and reheat in the microwave. Stir in the cream just before serving.

Per serving: Calories: 622; Total Fat: 40g; Saturated Fat: 15g; Cholesterol: 231mg; Sodium: 1,176mg; Total Carbohydrates: 12g; Sugars: 7g; Protein: 52g

THAI CHICKEN WITH COCONUT MILK

30 MINUTES OR LESS | **FREEZER-FRIENDLY** | **ONE POT**

SERVES 2 / PREP TIME: 5 MINUTES / COOK TIME: 15 MINUTES

This super-easy one-pot curry can be on the table in just about 20 minutes. Using a Thai curry paste, which is quite different from Indian curry pastes, gives it a distinctive flavor profile. The coconut milk adds both richness and depth. I recommend serving this dish over steamed rice.

1 TABLESPOON OLIVE OIL

1 SHALLOT, DICED

12 OUNCES BONELESS, SKINLESS CHICKEN BREAST OR THIGH, CUT INTO BITE-SIZE PIECES

1 TABLESPOON THAI RED CURRY PASTE

1 CUP COCONUT MILK

½ TEASPOON KOSHER SALT

¼ TEASPOON FRESHLY GROUND BLACK PEPPER

JUICE OF ½ LIME

1. In a medium skillet, heat the oil over medium-high heat. Add the shallot and cook, stirring, for about 5 minutes, until softened.

2. Add the chicken and cook, stirring occasionally, for about 5 minutes, until the chicken is cooked through.

3. Stir in the curry paste and cook for about 30 seconds, until fragrant.

4. Stir in the coconut milk and bring to a gentle boil. Cook for about 5 minutes more, until the sauce thickens. Season with the salt and pepper.

5. Just before serving, stir in the lime juice and serve hot.

Optional Finishing Touch: Garnish with chopped fresh cilantro, basil, or both.

Variation: Before serving, stir 2 cups fresh spinach and 2 tablespoons chopped fresh basil into the skillet. Cook until the spinach wilts.

Storage Tip: This dish freezes well. Cook it according to the instructions through step 4. Let cool to room temperature, then transfer it to a freezer-safe storage container and store in the freezer for up to 3 months. To serve, thaw in the refrigerator overnight and reheat in the microwave. Stir in the lime juice just before serving.

Per serving: Calories: 516; Total Fat: 38g; Saturated Fat: 23g; Cholesterol: 109mg; Sodium: 974mg; Total Carbohydrates: 8g; Sugars: 0g; Protein: 39g

PASTA WITH CHICKEN, TOMATOES, AND FETA

30 MINUTES OR LESS

SERVES 2 / PREP TIME: 5 MINUTES / COOK TIME: 25 MINUTES

Pasta is a great go-to easy dinner, but marinara or Bolognese sauce can get routine. This pasta dish is almost as easy to make and shakes things up in the flavor department. The best part: It only takes about 20 minutes from start to finish.

8 OUNCES FETTUCINE, LINGUINE, OR SPAGHETTI

1 TABLESPOON OLIVE OIL

2 BONELESS, SKINLESS CHICKEN BREAST FILLETS (ABOUT 12 OUNCES TOTAL)

½ TEASPOON KOSHER SALT

¼ TEASPOON FRESHLY GROUND BLACK PEPPER

1 (14-OUNCE) CAN DICED TOMATOES WITH ITALIAN SEASONING

½ CUP CRUMBLED FETA CHEESE, DIVIDED

2 TABLESPOONS CHOPPED FRESH BASIL

1. Bring a medium pot of water to a boil and cook the fettucine according to the package directions until al dente. Drain and set aside.

2. Meanwhile, in a medium skillet, heat the oil over medium-high heat.

3. Season the chicken with the salt and pepper, then add it to the pan. Cook until browned on the bottom, about 6 minutes. Turn the chicken over and cook for about 4 minutes more, until the chicken is cooked through.

4. Add the tomatoes and their juices. Cover the skillet and cook for about 10 minutes.

5. Stir all but 2 tablespoons of the cheese into the sauce, then cook for 5 more minutes, uncovered, until the sauce thickens.

6. Serve the chicken and sauce over the cooked pasta, garnished with the remaining 2 tablespoons cheese and the basil.

Optional Finishing Touch: Garnish with toasted pine nuts and grated Parmesan cheese.

Variation: For a different take on the dish and some extra vegetables, stir 3 cups fresh spinach into the sauce along with the feta.

Per serving: Calories: 820; Total Fat: 21g; Saturated Fat: 7g; Cholesterol: 142mg; Sodium: 1,219mg; Total Carbohydrates: 97g; Sugars: 11g; Protein: 58g

SOY-GINGER GLAZED CHICKEN

**SERVES 2 / PREP TIME: 5 MINUTES, PLUS 30 MINUTES
TO MARINATE / COOK TIME: 15 MINUTES**

A mixture of soy sauce, brown sugar, garlic, and ginger serves as both the marinade and sticky glaze for this simple chicken dish. Serve it over steamed rice with a side of broccoli or bok choy for a simple, healthy, and delicious weeknight meal.

¼ CUP PACKED
BROWN SUGAR

3 TABLESPOONS SOY SAUCE

1 TABLESPOON MINCED
FRESH GINGER OR
GINGER PASTE

2 TABLESPOONS
VEGETABLE OIL, DIVIDED

2 GARLIC CLOVES, MINCED

FRESHLY GROUND
BLACK PEPPER

2 TO 4 BONELESS, SKINLESS
CHICKEN THIGHS (ABOUT
12 OUNCES TOTAL)

1. In a medium bowl, whisk together the sugar, soy sauce, ginger, 1 tablespoon of the oil, the garlic, and pepper. Scoop about ¼ cup of the marinade out of the bowl and reserve for later. Add the chicken to the bowl and toss to coat well. Cover and refrigerate for at least 30 minutes or up to overnight (refrigerate the reserved sauce mixture, too, if keeping overnight).

2. In a medium skillet, heat the remaining 1 tablespoon oil over medium-high heat. Remove the chicken from the marinade, discarding the marinade, and add the meat to the skillet. Cook for 5 to 7 minutes, until browned on the bottom. Flip the chicken over and cook until the second side is browned, about 5 minutes more. Transfer the chicken to a plate.

3. Add the reserved marinade mixture to the skillet and bring it to a boil over medium-high heat. Reduce the heat to medium and cook, stirring and scraping up any browned bits that have stuck to the bottom of the pan, for 3 to 5 minutes, until the sauce thickens.

4. Remove the skillet from the heat and return the chicken to the pan. Toss the chicken to coat it well in the sauce. Serve hot.

Optional Finishing Touch: Garnish with thinly sliced scallions, toasted sesame seeds, or both.

Storage Tip: This dish freezes well. After cooking, let it cool to room temperature, then transfer it to a freezer-safe storage container and store in the freezer for up to 3 months. To serve, thaw in the refrigerator overnight and reheat in the microwave.

Per serving: Calories: 414; Total Fat: 21g; Saturated Fat: 3g; Cholesterol: 143mg; Sodium: 1,202mg; Total Carbohydrates: 23g; Sugars: 18g; Protein: 35g

TURKEY PICADILLO

30 MINUTES OR LESS **FREEZER-FRIENDLY** **ONE PAN**

SERVES 2 / PREP TIME: 5 MINUTES / COOK TIME: 15 MINUTES

This Cuban-style mixture is usually made with ground beef, but using turkey makes it a bit lighter. Serve it over rice or use it as a taco or burrito filling.

1 TABLESPOON OLIVE OIL

2 TABLESPOONS
  CHOPPED ONION

1 POUND GROUND TURKEY

½ CUP TOMATO SAUCE

¼ CUP SLICED
  PIMIENTO-STUFFED
  OLIVES, PLUS
  2 TEASPOONS BRINE
  FROM JAR

2 TABLESPOONS RAISINS

1. In a medium skillet, heat the oil over medium-high heat. Add the onion and cook, stirring, for about 5 minutes, until softened. Add the turkey and cook, breaking up the meat with a spatula, until browned, about 5 minutes more.

2. Add the tomato sauce, olives and brine, and raisins to the skillet and stir to combine. Bring the mixture to a boil, reduce the heat to medium, and let simmer, uncovered, until the sauce thickens a bit and the raisins have plumped up, about 5 minutes more. Serve hot.

Optional Finishing Touch: Garnish with chopped fresh cilantro.

Variation: A small minced clove of garlic and half a chopped bell pepper can be added along with the onion for a twist on the dish.

Storage Tip: This dish freezes well. After cooking, let it cool to room temperature, transfer it to a freezer-safe storage container, and store in the freezer for up to 3 months. To serve, thaw in the refrigerator overnight and reheat in the microwave.

Per serving: Calories: 416; Total Fat: 17g; Saturated Fat: 2g; Cholesterol: 124mg; Sodium: 846mg; Total Carbohydrates: 13g; Sugars: 8g; Protein: 54g

GREEK TURKEY BURGERS

30 MINUTES OR LESS   **FREEZER-FRIENDLY**

SERVES 2 / PREP TIME: 5 MINUTES / COOK TIME: 8 MINUTES

Ground turkey is great for making burgers. Lighter than their beef counterparts, turkey burgers really let any flavors you add shine. These are studded with tangy feta cheese and herbs. Serve them as you would any burgers, on buns with your favorite fixings.

⅔ POUND GROUND TURKEY

3 TABLESPOONS CRUMBLED
  FETA CHEESE

1 TABLESPOON CHOPPED
  FRESH DILL, OR
  1 TEASPOON DRIED DILL

1 GARLIC CLOVE, MINCED

1 TEASPOON
  DRIED OREGANO

½ TEASPOON KOSHER SALT

½ TEASPOON FRESHLY
  GROUND BLACK PEPPER

NONSTICK COOKING SPRAY

1. In a medium bowl, combine the turkey, cheese, dill, garlic, oregano, salt, and pepper and mix well. If you use your hands to combine the ingredients, be careful not to overwork the mixture. Form the mixture into two patties.

2. Spray a grill or grill pan with cooking spray and heat to medium-high heat. Cook the burgers until they are cooked through and have grill marks on both sides, 6 to 8 minutes, depending on how thick you make them. Serve hot.

Pairing Tip: You can make a quick tzatziki sauce to top your burgers. Grate a peeled cucumber on the large holes of a box grater. Mix the shredded cucumber with ½ cup plain yogurt, ½ small grated garlic clove, and 1 tablespoon fresh dill or 1 teaspoon dried dill.

Storage Tip: You can opt to freeze one or both burger patties before cooking. Wrap them tightly in plastic wrap and freeze for up to 3 months. To serve, thaw in the refrigerator overnight and then cook as directed.

Per serving: Calories: 213; Total Fat: 6g; Saturated Fat: 3g; Cholesterol: 96mg; Sodium: 616mg; Total Carbohydrates: 2g; Sugars: 1g; Protein: 38g

Grilled Flank Steak with Chili Butter, page 120

Chapter Eight

MEAT

GRILLED FLANK STEAK WITH CHILI BUTTER

30 MINUTES OR LESS

SERVES 2 TO 3 / PREP TIME: 5 MINUTES, PLUS 5 MINUTES
TO REST / COOK TIME: 10 MINUTES

You can make this dish with your go-to chili paste. My favorite is gochujang—a Korean seasoning paste made from fermented red chiles. It is both spicy and full of umami. You can buy it in Asian grocery stores, in the international foods aisle of many supermarkets, or online.

2 TABLESPOONS UNSALTED
BUTTER, AT ROOM
TEMPERATURE

2 TEASPOONS RED
CHILI PASTE

1 GARLIC CLOVE, PEELED

1 TEASPOON HONEY

¾ TEASPOON KOSHER
SALT, DIVIDED

½ TEASPOON FRESHLY
GROUND BLACK
PEPPER, DIVIDED

1 FLANK STEAK (ABOUT
1 POUND)

OLIVE OIL, FOR COATING
THE GRILL

1. In a food processor, combine the butter, the chili paste, garlic, honey, ¼ teaspoon of the salt, and ¼ teaspoon of the pepper and process until smooth and well combined.

2. Season the steak with the remaining ½ teaspoon salt and ¼ teaspoon pepper.

3. Heat a grill or grill pan over medium-high heat and lightly coat it with oil.

4. Grill the steak for 4 to 5 minutes, until grill marks appear on the bottom. Turn the steak over and grill until the meat is cooked to your desired doneness, about 3 minutes more for medium-rare.

5. Remove the steak from the grill, top it with the butter, and let it rest for at least 5 minutes.

6. Cut the steak across the grain into ⅛-inch-thick slices. Serve immediately.

Variation: If you don't have chili paste on hand, you can substitute 1 tablespoon red pepper flakes mixed with a dash of soy sauce, or use harissa.

Pairing Tip: I like to serve the sliced steak over a bed of salad greens or alongside roasted or mashed potatoes.

Per serving: Calories: 501; Total Fat: 31g; Saturated Fat: 15g; Cholesterol: 186mg; Sodium: 1,122mg; Total Carbohydrates: 6g; Sugars: 4g; Protein: 49g

GREEK-STYLE MEATBALLS WITH FRESH MINT

30 MINUTES OR LESS · **FREEZER-FRIENDLY** · **ONE POT**

SERVES 2 TO 3 / PREP TIME: 10 MINUTES / COOK TIME: 20 MINUTES

These tasty meatballs are studded with garlic and fresh mint. They're great with pasta and tomato sauce, as a filling for a pita sandwich with tzatziki sauce, or even as a topping for a Greek salad.

12 OUNCES GROUND
  BEEF OR LAMB (OR A
  COMBINATION)
½ CUP PANKO
  BREAD CRUMBS
1 LARGE EGG
1 GARLIC CLOVE, MINCED
2 TABLESPOONS FINELY
  CHOPPED FRESH
  MINT LEAVES
¾ TEASPOON KOSHER SALT
½ TEASPOON FRESHLY
  GROUND BLACK PEPPER
1 TABLESPOON OLIVE
  OIL, PLUS ADDITIONAL
  AS NEEDED

1. In a medium bowl, combine the beef, bread crumbs, egg, garlic, mint, salt, and pepper and mix well.

2. Form the meat mixture into golf-ball-size balls. You should get 16 to 18 meatballs.

3. In a medium skillet, heat the oil over medium-high heat. Cook the meatballs in the skillet, turning occasionally, until they are browned on all sides. They'll take 8 to 10 minutes to cook through, and you'll likely need to cook them in two batches. Add additional oil to the skillet as needed. Serve hot.

Storage Tip: These meatballs freeze well. Once cooked, arrange them in a single layer on a parchment paper–lined baking sheet and freeze. Transfer the frozen meatballs to a freezer-safe resealable plastic bag and store in the freezer for up to 3 months. To serve, thaw them overnight in the refrigerator and reheat in a skillet or the oven or microwave them in a covered bowl for 3 to 4 minutes.

Per serving: Calories: 532; Total Fat: 36g; Saturated Fat: 12g; Cholesterol: 205mg; Sodium: 932mg; Total Carbohydrates: 17g; Sugars: 1g; Protein: 37g

THAI BEEF SATAY

**SERVES 2 / PREP TIME: 10 MINUTES, PLUS 1 HOUR
TO MARINATE / COOK TIME: 5 MINUTES**

Often a good Thai-style dish requires a long list of ingredients. This one is simple but loaded with distinctive Thai flavor that's just as good as takeout.

¼ CUP FRESHLY SQUEEZED
   LIME JUICE
2 TABLESPOONS LIGHT
   BROWN SUGAR
2 TABLESPOONS
   FISH SAUCE
2 GARLIC CLOVES, MINCED
12 OUNCES FLANK STEAK,
   SLICED ACROSS THE
   GRAIN INTO ¼-INCH-
   THICK SLICES

1. In a medium bowl, stir together the lime juice, sugar, fish sauce, and garlic.

2. Add the steak and toss to coat. Cover and refrigerate for at least an hour or up to overnight.

3. Heat a grill or grill pan to medium heat.

4. Thread the meat slices onto skewers (with long skewers, you can probably do 2 or 3 per skewer).

5. Grill the meat for 2 to 3 minutes per side, until cooked to your desired doneness. Serve immediately.

Pairing Tip: Make a quick peanut dipping sauce by stirring together ¼ cup smooth peanut butter with ¼ cup warm water. Add 1½ teaspoons soy sauce and 1 teaspoon each minced fresh ginger, brown sugar, and chili paste.

Per serving: Calories: 312; Total Fat: 12g; Saturated Fat: 6g; Cholesterol: 114mg; Sodium: 1,390mg; Total Carbohydrates: 12g; Sugars: 10g; Protein: 37g

BEEF STROGANOFF

30 MINUTES OR LESS   **ONE PAN**

SERVES 2 / PREP TIME: 5 MINUTES / COOK TIME: 20 MINUTES

In this classic stroganoff, tender beef strips are seared in a skillet, then tossed with a sauce of sour cream and beef broth and served over egg noodles.

4 OUNCES EGG NOODLES

1 TABLESPOON OLIVE OIL

8 OUNCES TOP SIRLOIN, CUT INTO STRIPS

½ TEASPOON KOSHER SALT, DIVIDED

¼ TEASPOON FRESHLY GROUND BLACK PEPPER

¾ CUP PLUS 2 TABLESPOONS BEEF BROTH

¼ CUP SOUR CREAM

2 TABLESPOONS MINCED FRESH PARSLEY

1. Bring a medium pot of water to a boil and cook the noodles according to the package directions. Drain and set aside.

2. Meanwhile, in a medium skillet, heat the oil over medium-high heat. Add the beef and season it with ¼ teaspoon of the salt and the pepper. Cook, stirring occasionally, for about 5 minutes, until the beef is browned and cooked through. Transfer the meat to a plate.

3. Add the broth and sour cream to the skillet and stir to combine. Return the meat to the pan and cook for about 12 minutes, until the sauce thickens. Season with the remaining ¼ teaspoon salt.

4. Serve the meat and sauce spooned over the noodles, garnished with the parsley.

Variation: After browning the beef and removing it from the pan, you can add 6 ounces sliced mushrooms and cook, stirring, for about 8 minutes, until softened. Add the mushrooms to the plate with the browned beef and return them to the skillet at the same time.

Per serving: Calories: 499; Total Fat: 20g; Saturated Fat: 5g; Cholesterol: 71mg; Sodium: 747mg; Total Carbohydrates: 43g; Sugars: 1g; Protein: 36g

BEEF AND BEAN CHILI

30 MINUTES OR LESS **FREEZER-FRIENDLY** **ONE POT**

SERVES 2 / PREP TIME: 5 MINUTES / COOK TIME: 15 MINUTES

Sometimes a bowl of chili is the only thing that will satisfy. This easy version freezes well, so you might want to double the recipe and save half for another time.

8 OUNCES GROUND BEEF

½ ONION, DICED

1 (14.5-OUNCE) CAN DICED TOMATOES WITH GREEN CHILES

1 (15-OUNCE) CAN PINTO BEANS, DRAINED AND RINSED

2 TABLESPOONS CHILI POWDER (PAGE 160) OR STORE-BOUGHT

1. Heat a medium saucepan or Dutch oven over medium-high heat. Cook the beef, stirring and breaking it up with a spatula, for about 5 minutes, until browned. Transfer the meat to a plate and drain off all but about 1 tablespoon of the fat left in the skillet.

2. Add the onion to the pan and cook, stirring occasionally, for about 5 minutes, until softened.

3. Stir in the tomatoes and their juices, beans, and chili powder, and add the beef and any accumulated juices back to the pot. Cook for about 5 minutes more, until the beef is hot and the sauce has thickened. Serve hot.

Optional Finishing Touch: Serve garnished with shredded cheese, sour cream, chopped fresh cilantro, hot sauce or salsa, tortilla chips, and any other chili toppings you like.

Storage Tip: Chili freezes very well. Store in a freezer-safe covered container or resealable plastic bag in the freezer for up to 3 months. To serve, thaw overnight in the refrigerator and reheat on the stovetop or in the microwave.

Per serving: Calories: 508; Total Fat: 19g; Saturated Fat: 7g; Cholesterol: 75mg; Sodium: 655mg; Total Carbohydrates: 50g; Sugars: 11g; Protein: 37g

STEAK TACOS

**SERVES 2 / PREP TIME: 5 MINUTES, PLUS 5 MINUTES
TO REST / COOK TIME: 10 MINUTES**

A good flank steak doesn't need anything more than a sprinkling of chili powder to transform it into a delicious taco filling. Most chili powders contain a combination of ground chiles, paprika, cumin, and oregano; some contain garlic powder and other seasonings. You can make your own in large batches, so you always have it on hand, or simply find a store-bought version.

⅔ POUND FLANK STEAK

1 TABLESPOON OLIVE OIL

1 TABLESPOON CHILI
POWDER (PAGE 160)
OR STORE-BOUGHT

½ TEASPOON
GARLIC POWDER

½ TEASPOON KOSHER SALT

¼ TEASPOON FRESHLY
GROUND BLACK PEPPER

4 (7-INCH) CORN TORTILLAS

½ CUP SALSA

1. Rub the steak all over with the oil, then season with the chili powder, garlic powder, salt, and pepper.

2. Heat a grill or grill pan to medium-high heat.

3. Grill the steak for 3 to 4 minutes per side, until medium-rare.

4. Transfer the steak to a cutting board, tent loosely with aluminum foil, and let rest for 5 minutes.

5. Cut the steak across the grain into ¼-inch-thick slices.

6. Warm the tortillas for about 30 seconds per side either in a dry skillet over medium-high, directly over the burner on a gas stove, or on the grill.

7. Divide the steak among the tortillas, then top with the salsa and serve.

Optional Finishing Touch: Top your tacos with cheese—shredded Monterey Jack, Cheddar, crumbled feta, or queso fresco—along with chopped fresh cilantro, diced onions, and diced tomatoes.

Variation: Omit the tortilla and serve over rice or greens to turn this dish into a taco bowl.

Pairing Tip: This recipe is delicious served with Crunchy Apple and Cabbage Slaw (page 57).

Per serving: Calories: 444; Total Fat: 21g; Saturated Fat: 6g; Cholesterol: 102mg; Sodium: 978mg; Total Carbohydrates: 28g; Sugars: 3g; Protein: 36g

HUNGARIAN GOULASH

FREEZER-FRIENDLY **ONE POT**

SERVES 2 / PREP TIME: 5 MINUTES / COOK TIME: 1 HOUR 15 MINUTES

Traditional Hungarian goulash is a one-pot beef stew. A long simmer allows you to make great use of a tough but economical cut of beef. When the goulash is finished, the meat is fork-tender and deeply infused with the seasonings.

1 TABLESPOON OLIVE OIL

1 SMALL ONION, DICED

2 TABLESPOONS
  HUNGARIAN PAPRIKA

12 OUNCES BEEF STEW
  MEAT, CUT INTO
  1-INCH CUBES

1 CUP BEEF BROTH
  OR WATER

1 CUP CANNED DICED
  TOMATOES

½ TEASPOON KOSHER SALT

¼ TEASPOON FRESHLY
  GROUND BLACK PEPPER

1. In a large saucepan or Dutch oven, heat the oil over medium-high heat. Add the onion and cook, stirring occasionally, for about 5 minutes, until softened. Stir in the paprika and cook for about 30 seconds more.

2. Add the beef to the pot and cook, stirring occasionally, for about 5 minutes, until browned all over.

3. Add the broth and cook, stirring and scraping up any browned bits stuck to the bottom of the pan, for about 2 minutes. Stir in the tomatoes and their juices, salt, and pepper and bring to a boil.

4. Reduce the heat to low, cover, and simmer for about 1 hour, until the meat is very tender. Serve.

Optional Finishing Touch: Garnish with minced fresh flat-leaf parsley.

Pairing Tip: Goulash goes great with mashed potatoes.

Storage Tip: You can freeze goulash in a freezer-safe covered container or resealable plastic bag for up to 3 months. To serve, thaw overnight in the refrigerator and reheat on the stovetop or in the microwave.

Per serving: Calories: 356; Total Fat: 18g; Saturated Fat: 1g; Cholesterol: 81mg; Sodium: 512mg; Total Carbohydrates: 11g; Sugars: 5g; Protein: 39g

STIR-FRIED BEEF AND BROCCOLI IN HOISIN SAUCE

30 MINUTES OR LESS

SERVES 2 / PREP TIME: 5 MINUTES, PLUS 5 MINUTES TO REST / COOK TIME: 8 MINUTES

Why order takeout when you can make this delicious, healthy beef and broccoli dish at home in less than 20 minutes? Hoisin sauce is easy to find at any supermarket. It's sweet and savory and the perfect partner for beef.

12 OUNCES FLANK STEAK, THINLY SLICED

1 TABLESPOON SOY SAUCE

1 GARLIC CLOVE, MINCED

1 TABLESPOON VEGETABLE OIL

1 CUP SMALL BROCCOLI FLORETS

¼ CUP HOISIN SAUCE

1. In a medium bowl, toss the beef with the soy sauce and garlic.

2. In a large skillet, heat the oil over medium-high heat. Add the beef and cook for about 2 minutes, until browned. Transfer to a plate.

3. Add the broccoli to the skillet along with 2 tablespoons water. Cover and cook for 2 to 4 minutes, until the broccoli is crisp-tender.

4. Return the beef to the skillet, along with any accumulated juices. Add the hoisin sauce and cook, stirring, for 1 to 2 minutes. Serve hot.

Optional Finishing Touch: Garnish with toasted cashews and chopped fresh cilantro, or top with chili paste for some extra heat.

Flavor Tip: To boost the flavor in this dish, add 2 teaspoons minced fresh ginger with the garlic.

Pairing Tip: This dish tastes great served over steamed rice.

Per serving: Calories: 433; Total Fat: 22g; Saturated Fat: 7g; Cholesterol: 110mg; Sodium: 990mg; Total Carbohydrates: 18g; Sugars: 10g; Protein: 39g

SPICY PORK STIR-FRY

30 MINUTES OR LESS

SERVES 2 / PREP TIME: 5 MINUTES / COOK TIME: 7 MINUTES

Stir-fries are among the best dishes to make when you're cooking in small quantities. They're quick, require only a few ingredients, and are endlessly variable. Add vegetables and noodles or rice and this dish easily becomes a complete meal.

2 TABLESPOONS SOY SAUCE

1 TABLESPOON LIGHT BROWN SUGAR

1 TEASPOON GRATED FRESH GINGER OR GINGER PASTE

½ TEASPOON CHILI PASTE

1 TABLESPOON VEGETABLE OIL

12 OUNCES BONELESS PORK LOIN, CUT INTO ¼-INCH-THICK STRIPS

1. In a small bowl, mix together the soy sauce, sugar, ginger, and chili paste.

2. In a medium skillet, heat the oil over medium-high heat. Add the pork and cook, stirring, for about 5 minutes, until browned and cooked through.

3. Stir in the sauce mixture and cook for about 2 minutes, until the mixture bubbles and thickens. Serve hot.

Optional Finishing Touch: Garnish with chopped fresh cilantro or scallions.

Variation: Remove the pork from the skillet after browning and sauté ½ cup snow peas, ½ cup shredded carrots, and ½ cup sliced mushrooms before returning the pork to the pan.

Per serving: Calories: 274; Total Fat: 13g; Saturated Fat: 3g; Cholesterol: 98mg; Sodium: 912mg; Total Carbohydrates: 7g; Sugars: 5g; Protein: 31g

PULLED PORK SANDWICHES

FREEZER-FRIENDLY   **ONE POT**

**SERVES 2 / PREP TIME: 5 MINUTES /
COOK TIME: 2 HOURS 30 MINUTES TO 3 HOURS**

Pulled pork takes a few hours to cook, but the flavor makes it so worth it. This version uses sweet, caramel-colored soda as a braising liquid, which tenderizes the meat and gives it flavor. Make a double batch and freeze half for later. You won't regret it.

1¼ POUNDS BONELESS PORK
SHOULDER

1 TEASPOON KOSHER SALT

½ TEASPOON FRESHLY
GROUND BLACK PEPPER

1 TABLESPOON
VEGETABLE OIL

¾ CUP COLA

¾ CUP BARBECUE
SAUCE (PAGE 161) OR
STORE-BOUGHT

2 SANDWICH BUNS

½ CUP SHREDDED CABBAGE

1. Preheat the oven to 325°F.

2. Season the pork with the salt and pepper.

3. In an oven-safe pot, heat the oil over medium-high heat. Add the meat and cook for about 10 minutes total, turning every few minutes, until browned on all sides.

4. Remove the pot from the heat and pour the cola over the meat. Cover the pot and roast in the oven for 2 hours 30 minutes to 3 hours, until the pork shreds easily with a fork.

5. Remove the pork from the oven and let rest for 10 minutes.

6. Using two forks, shred the meat. Add the barbecue sauce and toss to coat.

7. Divide the pork equally between the two buns, and pile shredded cabbage on top. Serve immediately.

Storage Tip: Freeze the shredded cooked pork in barbecue sauce in a freezer-safe resealable plastic bag for up to 3 months. To serve, thaw in the refrigerator overnight and reheat on the stovetop or in the microwave.

Per serving: Calories: 963; Total Fat: 54g; Saturated Fat: 19g; Cholesterol: 175mg; Sodium: 2,212mg; Total Carbohydrates: 66g; Sugars: 36g; Protein: 52g

PORK CHILE VERDE

FREEZER-FRIENDLY

SERVES 2 TO 4 / PREP TIME: 5 MINUTES / COOK TIME: 2 HOURS 45 MINUTES

Chile verde is a classic dish that combines tangy tomatillos, spicy chiles, and hearty pork in a simple stew. You won't believe how easy it is to make. Serve it as a stew over Mexican- or Spanish-style rice or as a taco filling with warm corn tortillas.

12 OUNCES TOMATILLOS, PAPERY SKINS REMOVED, AND HALVED

2 GARLIC CLOVES, UNPEELED

½ CUP CHOPPED FRESH CILANTRO, PLUS ADDITIONAL FOR GARNISH

1 (3.5-OUNCE) CAN FIRE-ROASTED MILD GREEN CHILES DRAINED, (OPTIONAL)

2 TABLESPOONS OLIVE OIL

1½ POUNDS PORK SHOULDER, CUT INTO 2-INCH PIECES

1 TEASPOON KOSHER SALT

1½ TEASPOONS FRESHLY GROUND BLACK PEPPER

1. Preheat the broiler on high.

2. On a baking sheet, arrange the tomatillos, cut-side down, and the garlic and broil for about 5 minutes, until the tomatillo skins begin to blacken.

3. Peel the garlic and transfer it and the tomatillos to a blender. Add the cilantro and chiles (if using). Puree until smooth.

4. In a large skillet, heat the oil over medium-high heat. Season the pork all over with the salt and pepper and add it to the skillet. Cook, turning a few times, for about 5 minutes, until the meat is browned on all sides.

5. Once all the meat is browned, add the tomatillo mixture and 1¼ cups water and bring to a boil. Reduce the heat to low and simmer, uncovered, for about 2 hours 30 minutes, until the pork is very tender.

6. Serve hot, garnished with cilantro.

Pairing Tip: Serve over rice and top with crumbled queso fresco or feta cheese. You can also offer warm tortillas alongside the stew.

Storage Tip: Freeze the pork and sauce in a freezer-safe resealable plastic bag for up to 3 months. To serve, thaw in the refrigerator overnight and reheat on the stovetop or in the microwave.

Per serving: Calories: 570; Total Fat: 29g; Saturated Fat: 7g; Cholesterol: 195mg; Sodium: 1,867mg; Total Carbohydrates: 11g; Sugars: 0g; Protein: 65g

SAUSAGE WITH CARAMELIZED CABBAGE AND ONIONS

30 MINUTES OR LESS   **ONE PAN**

SERVES 2 TO 4 / PREP TIME: 5 MINUTES / COOK TIME: 23 MINUTES

This recipe takes sausages and veggies to the next level by caramelizing the cabbage and onions. The vegetables become deliciously sweet, making them a great counterpoint to the smoky sausage. A splash of vinegar at the end cuts the fattiness of the meat.

2 TABLESPOONS OLIVE OIL

1 SMALL ONION,
  THINLY SLICED

½ HEAD CABBAGE,
  THINLY SLICED

1 GARLIC CLOVE, MINCED

½ TEASPOON KOSHER SALT

3 TO 4 LINKS KIELBASA OR
  OTHER SMOKED SAUSAGE,
  CUT INTO ROUNDS

1 TEASPOON BALSAMIC OR
  RED WINE VINEGAR

1. In a large skillet, heat the oil over medium-high heat. Add the onion and cook, stirring occasionally, for about 3 minutes, until it begins to soften.

2. Add the cabbage, garlic, and salt and reduce the heat to medium-low. Cook, stirring occasionally, for about 15 minutes, until the cabbage and onion are very soft and golden brown.

3. Add the sausage and cook, stirring, for about 5 more minutes, until browned and heated through.

4. Remove the skillet from the heat and stir in the vinegar. Serve immediately.

Pairing Tip: This dish is great served over mashed potatoes.

Per serving: Calories: 435; Total Fat: 34g; Saturated Fat: 9g; Cholesterol: 78mg; Sodium: 1,764mg; Total Carbohydrates: 19g; Sugars: 7g; Protein: 17g

CIDER AND DIJON ROASTED PORK

FEELING FANCY **ONE PAN**

**SERVES 2 TO 4 / PREP TIME: 5 MINUTES, PLUS 5 MINUTES
TO REST / COOK TIME: 40 MINUTES**

Pork roast is worthy of special occasions. This one is seasoned with apple cider and Dijon mustard, giving it a sweet and savory flavor. Double this recipe because the leftovers are great for making sandwiches the next day.

2 TABLESPOONS
   VEGETABLE OIL

1 POUND BONELESS,
   CENTER-CUT PORK LOIN

½ TEASPOON KOSHER SALT

FRESHLY GROUND
   BLACK PEPPER

1 TABLESPOON APPLE
   CIDER VINEGAR

½ CUP APPLE CIDER

1 TABLESPOON
   DIJON MUSTARD

1 THYME SPRIG, OR
   1 TEASPOON DRIED THYME

1. Preheat the oven to 400°F.

2. In a large oven-safe skillet or Dutch oven, heat the oil over medium-high heat.

3. Season the pork with the salt and pepper, then add it to the skillet and cook, turning a few times, until browned on all sides, about 8 minutes total.

4. Mix together the vinegar, cider, and mustard and pour the mixture over the meat. Add the thyme to the pan. Transfer the pan to the oven and roast for 30 to 40 minutes, until the meat is cooked through.

5. Transfer the pork to a cutting board, tent it loosely with aluminum foil, and let it rest for at least 5 minutes.

6. Cut the meat across the grain into ½-inch-thick slices and serve immediately, with the pan drippings spooned over the top.

Flavor Tip: Sauté 1 or 2 diced apples or pears in butter with a pinch of salt and 1 teaspoon fresh thyme leaves. Spoon this mixture over the pork slices when serving.

Per serving: Calories: 541; Total Fat: 32g; Saturated Fat: 7g; Cholesterol: 150mg; Sodium: 638mg; Total Carbohydrates: 8g; Sugars: 7g; Protein: 48g

Blueberry Clafoutis,
page 144

Chapter Nine

DESSERTS

CHOCOLATE LAVA CAKES

SERVES 2 / PREP TIME: 5 MINUTES / COOK TIME: 12 MINUTES

Personal-size cakes that ooze a luscious dark chocolate filling from their centers—what more could you want? These are easy to make but never fail to impress.

3 TABLESPOONS
UNSALTED BUTTER,
PLUS ADDITIONAL FOR
GREASING THE RAMEKINS

3 TABLESPOONS
PLUS 2 TEASPOONS
SUGAR, DIVIDED

3 OUNCES DARK
CHOCOLATE,
FINELY CHOPPED

1 LARGE EGG

1 LARGE EGG YOLK

PINCH KOSHER SALT

3 TABLESPOONS FLOUR

1. Preheat the oven to 400°F.

2. Grease 2 (6-ounce) ramekins with butter, then sprinkle 1 teaspoon of the sugar into each of the ramekins. Shake the ramekins to distribute the sugar.

3. In a microwave-safe bowl, microwave the chocolate and butter together in 30-second intervals, stirring after each, until completely melted and smooth.

4. In a medium bowl, whisk together the egg, egg yolk, the remaining 3 tablespoons sugar, and the salt. Add the melted chocolate and stir to combine. Finally, add the flour and stir to incorporate.

5. Divide the batter equally between the prepared ramekins and place them on a baking sheet. Bake for 12 to 14 minutes, until the top is dry.

6. Remove the ramekins from the oven and let them cool for a couple of minutes before running a knife around the inside of the ramekins to loosen the cakes. Invert the cakes onto individual serving plates and serve.

Optional Finishing Touch: Garnish the cakes with fresh raspberries, lightly sweetened whipped cream, or both for extra goodness.

Variation: Substitute ¼ cup chocolate-hazelnut spread (like Nutella) for the chocolate. Melt it in the microwave with the butter for just about 30 seconds.

Per serving: Calories: 581; Total Fat: 37g; Saturated Fat: 22g; Cholesterol: 244mg; Sodium: 240mg; Total Carbohydrates: 55g; Sugars: 40g; Protein: 7g

RASPBERRY CRUMBLE

SERVES 2 / PREP TIME: 5 MINUTES / COOK TIME: 30 MINUTES

This sweet fruit crumble is proof that you only need a few simple ingredients to make a stunning dessert. You can even use frozen raspberries if fresh ones aren't available. A scoop of vanilla ice cream on top is optional but highly recommended.

½ CUP FLOUR, DIVIDED

½ CUP PACKED BROWN SUGAR, DIVIDED

¼ CUP OLD-FASHIONED ROLLED OATS

4 TABLESPOONS (½ STICK) BUTTER, AT ROOM TEMPERATURE

1½ CUPS RASPBERRIES

1. Preheat the oven to 350°F.

2. In a medium bowl, combine 6 tablespoons of the flour, 6 tablespoons of the sugar, the oats, and the butter. Mix with your hands until crumbly.

3. In a separate medium bowl, combine the remaining 2 tablespoons flour, 2 tablespoons sugar, and the raspberries and toss to coat the berries.

4. Spoon the raspberry mixture into 2 (6-ounce) ramekins. Sprinkle the crumb mixture over the top of the berries, dividing it equally between the ramekins.

5. Place the ramekins on a baking sheet and bake for 30 to 35 minutes, until the tops are golden brown and the raspberries are bubbling and syrupy. Serve warm.

Pairing Tip: Top the warm crumble with a scoop of creamy vanilla ice cream to make it even tastier.

Per serving: Calories: 540; Total Fat: 25g; Saturated Fat: 15g; Cholesterol: 61mg; Sodium: 176mg; Total Carbohydrates: 77g; Sugars: 40g; Protein: 6g

CHOCOLATE PEANUT BUTTER CRUNCH CUPS

MAKES 4 MINI CUPS / PREP TIME: 10 MINUTES, PLUS 30 MINUTES TO FREEZE / COOK TIME: 2 MINUTES

I don't need to tell you what a delicious combination chocolate and peanut butter is. These adorable little cups are easy to make. The rice cereal adds a pleasing crunch to the top layer of chocolate.

NONSTICK COOKING SPRAY

2 OUNCES DARK CHOCOLATE, FINELY CHOPPED

½ TEASPOON VEGETABLE OIL

3 TABLESPOONS PEANUT BUTTER

1½ TABLESPOONS POWDERED SUGAR

2 TABLESPOONS CRISPY RICE CEREAL

1. Line 4 mini-muffin cups with paper liners and coat the liners with cooking spray.

2. In a microwave-safe bowl, combine the chocolate and oil and microwave on high in 30-second intervals, stirring after each, until the chocolate is completely melted.

3. Place about 2 teaspoons of the chocolate mixture into the bottom of each cup, and tap the pan on the countertop a few times so that the chocolate spreads out and settles into the bottoms of the cups. Freeze for 10 minutes.

4. In a microwave-safe bowl, mix together the peanut butter and powdered sugar. Microwave for 20 to 30 seconds, until well combined and pourable. Spoon the peanut butter mixture into the cups on top of the first layer of chocolate, smoothing it into an even layer. Freeze for another 10 minutes.

⟶

5. Heat the remaining chocolate in the microwave in 30-second intervals, stirring after each, until it is melted again. Stir in the rice cereal, then spoon the mixture on top of the peanut butter, smoothing it into an even layer.

6. Freeze again for 10 minutes. Serve frozen.

Optional Finishing Touch: Sprinkle flaky sea salt on top of the final layer before freezing.

Variation: Use milk chocolate and almond or hazelnut butter instead of dark chocolate and peanut butter.

Per serving (1 mini cup): Calories: 168; Total Fat: 12g; Saturated Fat: 4g; Cholesterol: 0mg; Sodium: 55mg; Total Carbohydrates: 13g; Sugars: 10g; Protein: 4g

CINNAMON BREAD PUDDING

30 MINUTES OR LESS

SERVES 2 / PREP TIME: 5 MINUTES / COOK TIME: 25 MINUTES

Bread pudding has all the things you want in a dessert—it's gooey, sweet, rich, and flavorful—but it's deceptively easy to make. It's just a matter of tossing bread cubes with milk, eggs, and sugar and baking the mixture until it puffs up.

NONSTICK COOKING SPRAY OR VEGETABLE OIL

¼ CUP PLUS 2 TABLESPOONS REDUCED-FAT MILK

2 LARGE EGGS

2 TABLESPOONS SUGAR

3 CINNAMON BREAD SLICES (PREFERABLY SLIGHTLY STALE), CUT INTO CUBES

¼ CUP WHIPPED CREAM

1. Preheat the oven to 350°F. Grease 2 (8-ounce) ramekins with cooking spray.

2. In a medium bowl, whisk together the milk, eggs, and sugar. Add the bread cubes and toss to coat the bread well.

3. Spoon the mixture into the prepared ramekins, dividing it equally. Place the ramekins on a baking sheet.

4. Bake for 25 minutes, until the pudding puffs up and is set.

5. Serve hot, topped with the whipped cream.

Variation: If you don't have cinnamon bread, you can use regular sandwich bread and add ½ teaspoon ground cinnamon to the egg mixture.

Per serving: Calories: 347; Total Fat: 13g; Saturated Fat: 6g; Cholesterol: 205mg; Sodium: 290mg; Total Carbohydrates: 42g; Sugars: 22g; Protein: 13g

BLUEBERRY CLAFOUTIS

SERVES 2 / PREP TIME: 5 MINUTES / COOK TIME: 30 MINUTES

Clafoutis sound fancy even though they're crazy easy to make. Just create a layer of fresh fruit, pour a simple pancake-like batter over the top, and bake. The result is a cross between a custard and a thick, fruity pancake.

NONSTICK COOKING SPRAY
OR VEGETABLE OIL

1 CUP FRESH OR FROZEN
BLUEBERRIES

1 LARGE EGG

3 TABLESPOONS
REDUCED-FAT MILK

3 TABLESPOONS FLOUR

2 TABLESPOONS SUGAR

PINCH KOSHER SALT

1. Preheat the oven to 375°F. Lightly coat 2 (8-ounce) ramekins with cooking spray. Place the ramekins on a baking sheet.

2. Divide the berries evenly between the ramekins, placing them in an even layer.

3. In a medium bowl, whisk together the egg, milk, flour, sugar, and salt. Pour the mixture over the berries in the ramekins, dividing it equally.

4. Bake for 30 minutes, until the top is golden and the center is set.

Optional Finishing Touch: Garnish with a sprinkle of powdered sugar.

Variation: You can make clafoutis with any fruit you like. Cherries are the most traditional, but you can also use sliced strawberries, peaches, pears, or nectarines.

Per serving: Calories: 177; Total Fat: 3g; Saturated Fat: 1g; Cholesterol: 94mg; Sodium: 123mg; Total Carbohydrates: 33g; Sugars: 21g; Protein: 6g

CHOCOLATE MOUSSE

FEELING FANCY

**SERVES 2 / PREP TIME: 10 MINUTES, PLUS AT LEAST
2 HOURS TO CHILL / COOK TIME: 2 MINUTES**

This classic mousse is sweet but not too sweet. Dark chocolate brings bittersweet notes, and a shot of coffee adds another layer of bitterness to balance the sugar.

¼ CUP COLD HEAVY
(WHIPPING) CREAM
2 LARGE EGGS, SEPARATED
2 TABLESPOONS BREWED
COFFEE, AT ROOM
TEMPERATURE
1½ TABLESPOONS
SUGAR, DIVIDED
PINCH KOSHER SALT
3 OUNCES DARK
CHOCOLATE,
FINELY CHOPPED

1. In a small bowl, beat the cream until it holds stiff peaks. Cover with plastic wrap and refrigerate.

2. In the top of a double boiler over simmering water, whisk the egg yolks, coffee, 1 tablespoon of the sugar, and the salt for 1 to 2 minutes, until the mixture doubles in volume and is hot to the touch.

3. Remove the bowl or pot from the heat and whisk in the chocolate until it is completely melted and the mixture is smooth. Cool to room temperature.

4. In a separate medium bowl, beat the egg whites until they are foamy, then, with the mixer running, add the remaining ½ tablespoon sugar and beat until the mixture holds stiff peaks.

5. Gently fold the beaten egg whites into the chocolate mixture, then fold in the chilled whipped cream until just blended. Spoon the mixture into 2 (6-ounce) ramekins. Chill in the refrigerator for at least 2 hours. Serve chilled.

Optional Finishing Touch: Top with whipped cream, fresh raspberries or sliced strawberries, and shaved dark chocolate curls for added decadence.

Per serving: Calories: 450; Total Fat: 31g; Saturated Fat: 17g; Cholesterol: 227mg; Sodium: 159mg; Total Carbohydrates: 35g; Sugars: 28g; Protein: 8g

S'MORES COOKIE CUPS

30 MINUTES OR LESS

SERVES 2 / PREP TIME: 10 MINUTES / COOK TIME: 20 MINUTES

Sometimes it just isn't practical to build a campfire to make dessert. These s'mores cookie cups are cooked indoors, but they have all the flavors of a classic s'more—graham crackers, toasted marshmallows, and melty chocolate.

NONSTICK COOKING SPRAY OR BUTTER

3½ GRAHAM CRACKERS (WHOLE SHEETS)

2 TABLESPOONS UNSALTED BUTTER, MELTED

1 (1.55-OUNCE) BAR MILK CHOCOLATE (OR DARK CHOCOLATE), BROKEN INTO SEVERAL PIECES

½ CUP MINI MARSHMALLOWS

⅓ CUP SWEETENED CONDENSED MILK

1. Preheat the oven to 350°F. Lightly coat 2 (6-ounce) ramekins or muffin cups with cooking spray. If using ramekins, place them on a baking sheet.

2. In a food processor, pulse the graham crackers until they form coarse crumbs. Add the melted butter and pulse until the crumbs are fully moistened.

3. Divide the crumbs equally between the ramekins and press them down into an even layer.

4. Arrange the chocolate on top of the crumb layer, dividing it equally between the ramekins.

5. Top each with half the marshmallows, then pour half the sweetened condensed milk over the top.

6. Bake for about 20 minutes, until bubbling and golden brown on top.

7. Let cool before sliding a knife around the edges of each ramekin and lifting the cookie out of the cup. Serve warm or at room temperature.

Pairing Tip: For extra decadence, serve these cookie cups with steaming cups of hot chocolate.

Per serving: Calories: 508; Total Fat: 25g; Saturated Fat: 14g; Cholesterol: 53mg; Sodium: 324mg; Total Carbohydrates: 65g; Sugars: 51g; Protein: 8g

LEMON BUTTER CAKES

30 MINUTES OR LESS

SERVES 2 / PREP TIME: 5 MINUTES / COOK TIME: 20 MINUTES

These simple little cakes are based on a Dutch butter cake. They are kissed with lemon flavor, making them a ray of sunshine for a chilly winter day. Substitute vanilla extract for the lemon extract if you prefer.

NONSTICK COOKING SPRAY
OR BUTTER

½ CUP FLOUR

4 TABLESPOONS
(½ STICK) UNSALTED
BUTTER, MELTED

2½ TABLESPOONS
SUGAR

1 TEASPOON GRATED
LEMON ZEST

¼ TEASPOON
LEMON EXTRACT

PINCH KOSHER SALT

1. Preheat the oven to 350°F. Spray 2 (6-ounce) ramekins with cooking spray. Place the ramekins on a baking sheet.

2. In a small bowl, stir together the flour, butter, sugar, lemon zest, lemon extract, and salt to combine. Press the mixture into the prepared ramekins.

3. Bake for 18 to 20 minutes, until the cakes are golden brown around the edges but still gooey in the center.

4. Place the ramekins on a wire rack and let them cool before sliding a knife around the edges and lifting the cakes out of the ramekins. Serve warm or at room temperature.

Pairing Tip: These go well with fresh berries and lightly sweetened whipped cream.

Per serving: Calories: 369; Total Fat: 24g; Saturated Fat: 15g; Cholesterol: 61mg; Sodium: 242mg; Total Carbohydrates: 37g; Sugars: 13g; Protein: 4g

VANILLA FLAN

**SERVES 2 / PREP TIME: 15 MINUTES, PLUS OVERNIGHT
TO CHILL / COOK TIME: 30 MINUTES**

Flan was one of my mother's specialties, and I was always impressed by the caramel sauce that runs down the silky custard when it is unmolded. I think my version is every bit as good as hers.

¼ CUP PLUS 1 TABLESPOON
   SUGAR, DIVIDED

¼ CUP HEAVY
   (WHIPPING) CREAM

¼ CUP REDUCED-FAT MILK

2 LARGE EGG YOLKS

¼ TEASPOON
   VANILLA EXTRACT

1. Preheat the oven to 350°F.

2. In a small saucepan, heat ¼ cup of the sugar over low heat until it is fully melted and golden brown. Pour it into 2 (6-ounce) ramekins. Tip the ramekins to coat the bottoms completely with the syrup.

3. In a small bowl, beat the remaining 1 tablespoon sugar with the cream, milk, egg yolks, and vanilla.

4. Transfer the cream mixture to the ramekins. Place the ramekins in a baking dish, then fill the baking dish with 1 inch of boiling water. Place in the oven and bake for 30 to 35 minutes, until set.

5. Let cool to room temperature, then chill in the refrigerator overnight.

6. To serve, let the custards come to room temperature, then slide a knife around the edge of the custard and invert it onto a serving plate. The syrup will run down the sides of the flan, creating a sauce. Serve immediately.

Flavor Tip: Add ½ teaspoon ground cinnamon to the custard mixture for a hit of spice.

Per serving: Calories: 283; Total Fat: 16g; Saturated Fat: 9g; Cholesterol: 252mg; Sodium: 33mg; Total Carbohydrates: 34g; Sugars: 32g; Protein: 4g

NO-BAKE GINGER-LEMON TARTLETS

SERVES 2 / PREP TIME: 10 MINUTES, PLUS 4 HOURS TO CHILL

A crunchy gingersnap-crumb crust makes the perfect base for the tart and sweet filling, which is made with sour cream and lemon curd. This no-bake dessert is easy to make ahead of time.

½ CUP GINGERSNAP
   CRUMBS

1 TABLESPOON UNSALTED
   BUTTER, MELTED

¼ CUP SOUR CREAM

¼ CUP LEMON CURD

¼ CUP SWEETENED
   WHIPPED CREAM

1. In a small bowl, mix together the cookie crumbs and melted butter. Press the crumb mixture into the bottom and up the sides of 2 (6-ounce) ramekins.

2. In another small bowl, whisk the sour cream until it fluffs up. Add the lemon curd and whisk to incorporate.

3. Spoon the sour cream mixture into the prepared crusts. Cover the tartlets and chill for at least 4 hours.

4. Serve chilled, topped with the whipped cream.

Optional Finishing Touch: Sprinkle minced candied ginger over the tops of the tartlets before serving.

Variation: Substitute graham cracker crumbs for the gingersnap crumbs.

Per serving: Calories: 380; Total Fat: 29g; Saturated Fat: 16g; Cholesterol: 137mg; Sodium: 355mg; Total Carbohydrates: 32g; Sugars: 15g; Protein: 5g

Fresh Salsa Picanta, page 162
Dry-Fried Green Beans, page 158

Chapter Ten

SNACKS, SIDES, AND STAPLES

NO-BAKE CHOCOLATE CHIP GRANOLA BARS

30 MINUTES OR LESS **FREEZER-FRIENDLY**

SERVES 2 / PREP TIME: 5 MINUTES, PLUS 20 MINUTES TO CHILL

Granola bars are a great on-the-go snack, and they are easy to make yourself.

¼ CUP PITTED DATES

1 TABLESPOON HONEY

1 TABLESPOON CRUNCHY
PEANUT BUTTER

¼ CUP GRANOLA

2 TABLESPOONS
MINI SEMISWEET
CHOCOLATE CHIPS

1. In a mini food processor, process the dates for about 1 minute, scraping down the sides as needed, until a paste forms.

2. In a small microwave-safe bowl, combine the honey and peanut butter and microwave for 15 to 30 seconds, then stir to mix.

3. Add the date paste, granola, and chocolate chips and stir to mix well.

4. Transfer the mixture to a sheet of plastic wrap and form it into a square about ½ inch thick. Wrap tightly and chill in the refrigerator for about 20 minutes. Cut in half to serve.

Variation: You can substitute almond butter for the peanut butter and toasted oats for the granola or add dried cherries or other fruit.

Storage Tip: Store in the freezer, wrapped tightly in plastic wrap, for up to 3 months.

Per serving: Calories: 247; Total Fat: 16g; Saturated Fat: 5g; Cholesterol: 0mg; Sodium: 45mg; Total Carbohydrates: 53g; Sugars: 38g; Protein: 7g

SPICY CANDIED PECANS

30 MINUTES OR LESS   **FREEZER-FRIENDLY**

SERVES 2 / PREP TIME: 5 MINUTES / COOK TIME: 10 MINUTES

Candied nuts are deliciously addictive as a snack. They also make a great topper for salads, adding flavor and crunchy texture. Sprinkle them over a salad of tender greens, any sort of fruit, blue cheese or goat cheese, and vinaigrette dressing.

2 TABLESPOONS
  POWDERED SUGAR

¼ TEASPOON GROUND
  CINNAMON

PINCH KOSHER SALT

PINCH CAYENNE PEPPER

PINCH GROUND NUTMEG

½ CUP PECANS

1. Preheat the oven to 350°F. Line a baking sheet with parchment paper.

2. In a small bowl, combine the sugar, 1 teaspoon water, the cinnamon, salt, cayenne, and nutmeg and mix well.

3. Add the pecans to the bowl and stir to coat.

4. Spread the nuts on the prepared baking sheet in a single layer. Bake for about 10 minutes, until the nuts are dark brown (be careful not to let them burn).

5. Remove the nuts from the pan immediately by transferring the parchment paper to a cooling rack. The sugar coating will harden as the nuts cool. Enjoy at room temperature.

Storage Tip: Candied nuts will keep in an airtight container at room temperature for up to a week. You can store them in a freezer-safe resealable plastic bag in the freezer for up to 3 months.

Per serving: Calories: 288; Total Fat: 23g; Saturated Fat: 2g; Cholesterol: 0mg; Sodium: 78mg; Total Carbohydrates: 20g; Sugars: 16g; Protein: 4g

ROASTED RED PEPPER HUMMUS

SERVES 2 / PREP TIME: 5 MINUTES / COOK TIME: 10 MINUTES

Hummus makes a great snack or sandwich filling. This one is flavored with roasted red peppers that you can buy in a jar or make yourself. Serve it with toasted pita triangles, pita chips, or raw vegetables for dipping.

1 CUP CANNED CHICKPEAS, DRAINED AND RINSED

2 TABLESPOONS OLIVE OIL

2 TABLESPOONS TAHINI

2 TABLESPOONS CHOPPED ROASTED RED PEPPERS

1 TABLESPOON FRESHLY SQUEEZED LEMON JUICE

1 SMALL GARLIC CLOVE, MINCED

In a mini food processor, combine the chickpeas, oil, tahini, red peppers, lemon juice, and garlic and process until smooth. Serve immediately.

Storage Tip: Hummus will keep covered in the refrigerator for up to 3 days.

Per serving: Calories: 359; Total Fat: 24g; Saturated Fat: 3g; Cholesterol: 0mg; Sodium: 206mg; Total Carbohydrates: 32g; Sugars: 1g; Protein: 9g

LEMONY QUINOA WITH TURMERIC

30 MINUTES OR LESS

SERVES 2 / PREP TIME: 5 MINUTES / COOK TIME: 15 MINUTES

This lemony grain salad is full of bright citrus flavor. It's heartier than a vegetable-only salad, and it makes a nice side for meat dishes or other entrées.

½ CUP UNCOOKED QUINOA

KOSHER SALT

2 TEASPOONS OLIVE OIL

2 TEASPOONS FRESHLY
 SQUEEZED LEMON JUICE

⅛ TEASPOON GROUND
 TURMERIC

FRESHLY GROUND
 BLACK PEPPER

6 CHERRY
 TOMATOES, HALVED

2 TABLESPOONS CRUMBLED
 FETA CHEESE

1. In a small saucepan, bring 1 cup water to a boil. Add the quinoa and a pinch of salt and reduce the heat to medium-low.

2. Cook for about 15 minutes, until the quinoa is tender and the water has been absorbed. Transfer the quinoa to a bowl and let cool.

3. In a small bowl, whisk together the oil, lemon juice, turmeric, and a pinch each of salt and pepper.

4. Add the tomatoes and the dressing to the quinoa and toss to mix. Sprinkle the cheese over the top and serve.

Optional Finishing Touch: Garnish with chopped fresh flat-leaf parsley.

Variation: Add halved, pitted Kalamata olives or chopped artichoke hearts along with the tomatoes, or add chickpeas to make it a more substantial dish.

Per serving: Calories: 232; Total Fat: 9g; Saturated Fat: 2g; Cholesterol: 8mg; Sodium: 188mg; Total Carbohydrates: 30g; Sugars: 2g; Protein: 8g

RICE PILAF WITH ALMONDS AND RAISINS

30 MINUTES OR LESS

SERVES 2 / PREP TIME: 5 MINUTES / COOK TIME: 25 MINUTES

Rice pilaf is a simple way to elevate a meal. Serve this alongside chicken, fish, or meat dishes.

1 TABLESPOON OLIVE OIL

2 TABLESPOONS
  DICED ONION

1 CUP BASMATI RICE

1 TABLESPOON
  SLIVERED ALMONDS

1 TABLESPOON RAISINS

1⅓ CUPS CHICKEN BROTH,
  VEGETABLE BROTH,
  OR WATER

½ TEASPOON KOSHER SALT

FRESHLY GROUND
  BLACK PEPPER

1. In a medium saucepan, heat the oil over medium-high heat. Cook the onion, stirring, for about 3 minutes, until softened. Add the rice and cook, stirring, until the grains are fully coated with oil and slightly translucent.

2. Stir in the almonds and raisins.

3. Stir in the broth and bring the mixture to a boil.

4. Reduce the heat to low, cover, and simmer for 15 to 20 minutes, until the rice is tender and the liquid has been fully absorbed. Season and serve hot.

Optional Finishing Touch: Garnish with chopped fresh flat-leaf parsley or cilantro.

Pairing Tip: Serve this rice pilaf alongside Cider and Dijon Roasted Pork (page 135).

Per serving: Calories: 432; Total Fat: 9g; Saturated Fat: 1g; Cholesterol: 0mg; Sodium: 426mg; Total Carbohydrates: 79g; Sugars: 3g; Protein: 8g

ROASTED BRUSSELS SPROUTS WITH PESTO AND PARMESAN

30 MINUTES OR LESS

SERVES 2 / PREP TIME: 5 MINUTES / COOK TIME: 20 MINUTES

Some people find Brussels sprouts bitter, but roasting mellows them, and coating them with herby pesto makes them irresistible.

8 OUNCES BRUSSELS
SPROUTS, TRIMMED AND
HALVED THROUGH THE
STEM END

1 TABLESPOON OLIVE OIL

¼ TEASPOON KOSHER SALT

¼ TEASPOON FRESHLY
GROUND BLACK PEPPER

2 TABLESPOONS HERB
PESTO, HOMEMADE
(PAGE 163) OR
STORE-BOUGHT

2 TABLESPOONS
FRESHLY GRATED
PARMESAN CHEESE

2 TABLESPOONS CRUSHED
ROASTED PISTACHIOS

1. Preheat the oven to 425°F.

2. In a medium bowl, toss together the Brussels sprouts, oil, salt, and pepper.

3. On a rimmed baking sheet, spread the Brussels sprouts in a single layer, cut-side down.

4. Roast for 20 to 25 minutes, until the sprouts are browned on the bottoms.

5. Transfer to a bowl (you can use the bowl you tossed them in before roasting) and toss them with the pesto.

6. Sprinkle the cheese and pistachios over the top and serve.

Pairing Tip: Serve alongside Italian-Style Oven-Baked Fish (page 93).

Per serving: Calories: 241; Total Fat: 19g; Saturated Fat: 4g; Cholesterol: 3mg; Sodium: 405mg; Total Carbohydrates: 14g; Sugars: 4g; Protein: 8g

DRY-FRIED GREEN BEANS

30 MINUTES OR LESS

SERVES 2 / PREP TIME: 5 MINUTES / COOK TIME: 20 MINUTES

This method for preparing green beans is inspired by the Chinese version that almost always includes ground pork. This vegetarian version makes a great side.

3 TABLESPOONS OLIVE OIL

8 OUNCES GREEN
  BEANS, HALVED

1 SCALLION, BOTH WHITE
  AND GREEN PARTS,
  THINLY SLICED

1 SMALL GARLIC
  CLOVE, MINCED

1 TEASPOON SUGAR

1 TABLESPOON SOY SAUCE

1. In a large skillet, warm the oil over medium-high heat until it shimmers.

2. Add the green beans and cook, stirring, for 3 to 4 minutes, until they are browned in spots.

3. Add the scallion and garlic and toss to combine. Add 1 teaspoon water and the sugar and cook until the water evaporates, about 1 minute more. Add the soy sauce and toss to coat. Serve hot.

Variation: Add a thinly sliced hot red chile to the pan along with the garlic for a bit of heat.

Per serving: Calories: 237; Total Fat: 21g; Saturated Fat: 2g; Cholesterol: 0mg; Sodium: 421mg; Total Carbohydrates: 12g; Sugars: 4g; Protein: 3g

PARMESAN GARLIC SMASHED POTATOES

SERVES 2 / PREP TIME: 5 MINUTES / COOK TIME: 35 MINUTES

These twice-cooked potatoes require a bit of patience as you wait for them first to be boiled until tender and then again as they bake to crispy, golden-brown perfection, but they are so worth it.

8 OUNCES SMALL YUKON
 GOLD POTATOES
KOSHER SALT
2 TABLESPOONS UNSALTED
 BUTTER, MELTED
1 GARLIC CLOVE, MINCED
FRESHLY GROUND
 BLACK PEPPER
¼ CUP FRESHLY GRATED
 PARMESAN CHEESE

1. Preheat the oven to 425°F.

2. Place the potatoes in a saucepan and cover them with water. Add a pinch of salt and bring to a boil. Cook until the potatoes are easily pierced with a fork, about 15 minutes. Drain and let cool for several minutes.

3. Transfer the potatoes to a rimmed baking sheet and drizzle with the melted butter. Add the garlic and toss to coat the potatoes well. Spread the potatoes into a single layer, then smash each one using the bottom of a glass jar or juice glass.

4. Season with salt and pepper, then sprinkle the cheese over the top.

5. Bake for about 25 minutes, until the cheese is golden brown and the potatoes are browned and crisp on the bottom.

Optional Finishing Touch: Sprinkle with sliced fresh chives just before serving.

Pairing Tip: Serve alongside Greek Lemon Chicken with Olives (page 99).

Per serving: Calories: 227; Total Fat: 15g; Saturated Fat: 9g; Cholesterol: 41mg; Sodium: 296mg; Total Carbohydrates: 19g; Sugars: 1g; Protein: 7g

CHILI POWDER

MAKES ABOUT ¾ CUP / PREP TIME: 5 MINUTES

Chili powder is a versatile seasoning. It provides flavor for numerous recipes in this book, and once you have a stash of it, you'll find yourself reaching for it time and again.

½ CUP SWEET PAPRIKA

2 TABLESPOONS
   GARLIC POWDER

1½ TABLESPOONS
   DRIED OREGANO

1½ TABLESPOONS
   GROUND CUMIN

1 TEASPOON
   CAYENNE PEPPER

In a small bowl, combine the paprika, garlic powder, oregano, cumin, and cayenne. Store in an airtight container in a cool, dark place.

Flavor Tip: Add a teaspoon of smoked paprika or ½ teaspoon ground chipotle chile for smoky flavor and, in the case of the chipotle, extra heat.

Per serving (1 tablespoon): Calories: 34; Total Fat: 1g; Saturated Fat: 0g; Cholesterol: 0mg; Sodium: 7mg; Total Carbohydrates: 6g; Sugars: 1g; Protein: 2g

BARBECUE SAUCE

30 MINUTES OR LESS

MAKES ABOUT 1¼ CUPS / PREP TIME: 5 MINUTES / COOK TIME: 5 MINUTES

A good barbecue sauce can turn even the simplest meal into party-worthy fare. Use this sauce on chicken, ribs, or pork. You can even use it as a sauce for a barbecue chicken pizza or Pulled Pork Sandwiches (page 131).

¾ CUP KETCHUP

⅓ CUP APPLE
   CIDER VINEGAR

¼ CUP PACKED
   BROWN SUGAR

1 TEASPOON KOSHER SALT

1 TEASPOON FRESHLY
   GROUND BLACK PEPPER

½ TEASPOON
   CAYENNE PEPPER

¼ TEASPOON GROUND
   CINNAMON

In a small saucepan, stir together the ketchup, vinegar, sugar, salt, pepper, cayenne, and cinnamon, and bring to a simmer over medium heat. Cook, stirring frequently, for 5 minutes, until the sauce thickens slightly. Use immediately or cool to room temperature and store for later use.

Variation: Add a splash of bourbon or hot sauce along with the other ingredients.

Storage Tip: Store in an airtight container in the refrigerator for up to a week or in the freezer for up to 3 months.

Per serving (¼ cup): Calories: 68; Total Fat: 0g; Saturated Fat: 0g; Cholesterol: 0mg; Sodium: 547mg; Total Carbohydrates: 17g; Sugars: 15g; Protein: 1g

FRESH SALSA PICANTE

MAKES ABOUT 1¼ CUPS / PREP TIME: 5 MINUTES

Sure, you can buy salsa at the supermarket, but it's so much more flavorful when it's made fresh. Use this spicy condiment on tacos and other Mexican-inspired dishes, or serve it as a dip for chips.

2 MEDIUM TOMATOES, QUARTERED

¼ ONION

¼ CUP FRESH CILANTRO LEAVES

1 SMALL JALAPEÑO PEPPER, STEMMED (SEEDED FOR A MILDER SALSA)

JUICE OF 1 LIME

¼ TEASPOON KOSHER SALT

In a food processor, combine the tomatoes, onion, cilantro, jalapeño, lime juice, and salt. Pulse to chop to a chunky texture.

Variation: Substitute fresh pineapple or mango for the tomatoes to make a tropical salsa.

Per serving (¼ cup): Calories: 14; Total Fat: 0g; Saturated Fat: 0g; Cholesterol: 0mg; Sodium: 119mg; Total Carbohydrates: 3g; Sugars: 2g; Protein: 1g

HERB PESTO

30 MINUTES OR LESS　　**FREEZER-FRIENDLY**

MAKES ABOUT ¾ CUP / PREP TIME: 5 MINUTES

Pesto is great on pasta, but it also serves as a flavorful sandwich spread or addition to sauces or salad dressings. When you find inexpensive fresh herbs, buy them in large quantities and make big batches of this pesto, which you can portion out in ice cube trays and freeze.

2 CUPS FRESH HERBS
(BASIL, CILANTRO,
PARSLEY, MINT, OR A
COMBINATION)

2 TABLESPOONS NUTS
(PINE NUTS, WALNUTS,
ALMONDS, OR
PISTACHIOS)

2 GARLIC CLOVES, PEELED

1 TEASPOON GRATED
LEMON ZEST

¼ TEASPOON KOSHER SALT

¼ TEASPOON FRESHLY
GROUND BLACK PEPPER

½ CUP OLIVE OIL

½ CUP GRATED
PARMESAN CHEESE

1. In a food processor, combine the herbs, nuts, garlic, lemon zest, salt, and pepper and process to a very fine mince.

2. With the food processor running, add the oil in a slow stream and process until the mixture is smooth and thick.

3. Add the cheese and process just to combine. Use immediately or store for later.

Storage Tip: Pesto will keep in a covered container in the refrigerator for up to 3 days or in the freezer for up to 3 months.

Per serving (2 tablespoons): Calories: 194; Total Fat: 20g; Saturated Fat: 4g; Cholesterol: 7mg; Sodium: 203mg; Total Carbohydrates: 2g; Sugars: 0g; Protein: 4g

SIMPLE VINAIGRETTE DRESSING

30 MINUTES OR LESS

MAKES ABOUT ¾ CUP / PREP TIME: 5 MINUTES

Once you start making your own salad dressing, it's hard to go back to the store-bought stuff. It's simple to make and you can control the ingredients, making sure there aren't any unnecessary additives. This one is extremely versatile—adjust it as you see fit and use it on all types of salads.

⅓ CUP VINEGAR (WINE, BALSAMIC, OR APPLE CIDER)

1 TABLESPOON FRESH HERBS (BASIL, OREGANO, THYME, CILANTRO, OR PARSLEY), OR 1 TEASPOON DRIED

1 TO 2 GARLIC CLOVES, MINCED

1½ TEASPOONS KOSHER SALT

1 TEASPOON DIJON MUSTARD

½ TEASPOON FRESHLY GROUND BLACK PEPPER

½ CUP OLIVE OIL

1. In a small bowl, whisk together the vinegar, herbs, garlic, salt, mustard, and pepper.

2. While whisking, slowly add the oil in a thin stream. Continue whisking until the mixture emulsifies.

Variation: Make a Ginger-Miso Dressing by using wine vinegar, substituting 2 teaspoons minced fresh ginger for the garlic and 1 teaspoon toasted sesame oil for the mustard, omitting the herbs and salt, and adding 2 tablespoons white miso paste.

Storage Tip: The vinaigrette will keep in an airtight container in the refrigerator for up to 2 weeks. If the oil solidifies, simply let the dressing come to room temperature and shake or whisk to emulsify again.

Per serving: Calories: 149; Total Fat: 17g; Saturated Fat: 2g; Cholesterol: 0mg; Sodium: 492mg; Total Carbohydrates: 1g; Sugars: 0g; Protein: 0g

MARINARA SAUCE

30 MINUTES OR LESS | **FREEZER-FRIENDLY**

MAKES ABOUT 2 CUPS / PREP TIME: 15 MINUTES

Adding butter to tomato sauce is a trick I learned from the great Italian chef Marcella Hazan. It adds richness and counterbalances the acidity of the tomatoes. This sauce is perfect on pasta or with Mushroom and Lentil Meatballs (page 78). Make a large batch and freeze it. You'll never buy jarred pasta sauce again.

¼ CUP OLIVE OIL

1 (28-OUNCE) CAN CRUSHED TOMATOES

3 GARLIC CLOVES, MINCED

½ TEASPOON KOSHER SALT

¼ TEASPOON FRESHLY GROUND BLACK PEPPER

2 TABLESPOONS UNSALTED BUTTER

1 TABLESPOON MINCED FRESH OREGANO OR 1 TEASPOON DRIED

PINCH SUGAR

1. In a medium saucepan, heat the oil over medium heat.

2. Add the tomatoes, garlic, salt, and pepper and bring to a boil. Cook, stirring frequently, for about 15 minutes, until the sauce thickens.

3. Stir in the butter, oregano, and sugar and remove from the heat. Use immediately or let cool and store for later use.

Storage Tip: This sauce will keep in a covered container in the refrigerator for up to 5 days or in the freezer for up to 3 months.

Per serving (½ cup): Calories: 246; Total Fat: 19g; Saturated Fat: 6g; Cholesterol: 15mg; Sodium: 513mg; Total Carbohydrates: 18g; Sugars: 11g; Protein: 5g

MEASUREMENT CONVERSIONS

VOLUME EQUIVALENTS (DRY)

US STANDARD	METRIC (APPROXIMATE)
⅛ teaspoon	0.5 mL
¼ teaspoon	1 mL
½ teaspoon	2 mL
¾ teaspoon	4 mL
1 teaspoon	5 mL
1 tablespoon	15 mL
¼ cup	59 mL
⅓ cup	79 mL
½ cup	118 mL
⅔ cup	156 mL
¾ cup	177 mL
1 cup	235 mL
2 cups or 1 pint	475 mL
3 cups	700 mL
4 cups or 1 quart	1 L
½ gallon	2 L
1 gallon	4 L

VOLUME EQUIVALENTS (LIQUID)

US STANDARD	US STANDARD (OUNCES)	METRIC (APPROXIMATE)
2 tablespoons	1 fl. oz.	30 mL
¼ cup	2 fl. oz.	60 mL
½ cup	4 fl. oz.	120 mL
1 cup	8 fl. oz.	240 mL
1½ cups	12 fl. oz.	355 mL
2 cups or 1 pint	16 fl. oz.	475 mL
4 cups or 1 quart	32 fl. oz.	1 L
1 gallon	128 fl. oz.	4 L

WEIGHT EQUIVALENTS

US STANDARD	METRIC (APPROXIMATE)
½ ounce	15 g
1 ounce	30 g
2 ounces	60 g
4 ounces	115 g
8 ounces	225 g
12 ounces	340 g
16 ounces or 1 pound	455 g

OVEN TEMPERATURES

FAHRENHEIT (F)	CELSIUS (C) (APPROXIMATE)
250°F	120°C
300°F	150°C
325°F	180°C
375°F	190°C
400°F	200°C
425°F	220°C
450°F	230°C

INDEX

ABOUT THE AUTHOR

Robin Donovan is a food writer, recipe developer, and author of numerous cookbooks, including the bestselling *Deceptively Easy Desserts* and *Dessert Cooking for Two*. She lives in Berkeley, California, and blogs about easy recipes for people who love food at AllWaysDelicious.com.